CATCH THE
MILLENNIUM
BUG
WITH ERIC AND

Co Down

Edited by Dave Thomas

First published in Great Britain in 1999 by
YOUNG WRITERS
Remus House, Coltsfoot Drive,
Woodston,
Peterborough, PE2 9JX
Telephone (01733) 890066

HB ISBN 0 75431 534 7
SB ISBN 0 75431 535 5

FOREWORD

Young Writers have produced poetry books in conjunction with schools for over eight years; providing a platform for talented young people to shine. This year, the Celebration 2000 collection of regional anthologies were developed with the millennium in mind.

With the nation taking stock of how far we have come, and reflecting on what we want to achieve in the future, our anthologies give a vivid insight into the thoughts and experiences of the younger generation.

We were once again impressed with the quality and attention to detail of every entry received and hope you will enjoy the poems we have decided to feature in *Celebration Co Down* for many years to come.

CONTENTS

Andrews Memorial Primary School

Andrew Bell	1
Lorna McGrady	1
Amber Davis	2
Kristofer Best	2
Suzanne Majury	2
Marc Wilson	3
Victoria Brown	3
Ryan Galway	4
Jane Bicker	4
Lauren Alexander	5
Gareth Eynon	5
Michelle Victoria Coey	6
Alison Fulford	6
Ryan Connolly	7
Rachel Scott	7
Graham Martin	8
Christopher McBride	8
Jenny Gouk	9
Caitlin Kirkwood	9
Allison Ferguson	10
Jeanine Davidson	10
Cara McDonald	10
Stuart Maguire	11
Victoria Savage	11
Christopher Napier	12
Glenn McKibbin	12
Rory Gibson	13
Sarah Hunter	14
Lynsey Gillespie	14
Stephen McBurney	15
Claire Caldwell	16
Sam Long	17

Ballyholme Primary School

Stephen Robinson	17
Adhamh Callan-Rushe	18
Louise Cochrane	18
Jenni McClelland	19
Danial Parker	19
David Thompson	20
Kirsty Mulholland	20
Lauren Morales	21
Amy Finch	22
Peter Irwin	22
Lauren Cheshire	23
Sarah Leinster	23
Sarah Coghlan	24
Erin Mullan	24
Edward Hewitt	25
Francesca Darrah	25
Zara Gilroy	26
Suzanna Clark	26

Ballyvester Primary School

Kerry Savage	27
Leona Wells	27
Roxanne Aicken	28
Jacqui Beattie	28
Laurie Symon	29
Claire Breadon	29
Ryan Lee	30
Laura Gourley	30

Cedar Integrated Primary School

Bronagh Clare Getty	31
Natalie Savage	31
Francesca Whaley	32
Catherine Speers	32
Mark Kirk	33
Caitlin Morrison	33
Emma Morgan	34

Stephen Cullum   34
Andrew Spence   35

Convent of Mercy Primary School
          Carrie Anne Crolly-Burton   35
          Emma Stranney   36
          Clara Keenan   36
          Janine McGrady   37
          Sarah Rice   37
          Catherine Dougherty   38
          Maria O'Hare   38
          Grainne Teggart   39
          Daena Walker   39
          Danielle McDowell   40
          Julie-Ann Rodgers   40
          Kathleen Ward   41
          Sarah McAuley   41
          Michelle Murray   41
          Laura Polly   42
          Rebecca Gribben   42
          Lisa Totten   43
          Nathanya McColl   43
          Ciara Vance   44
          Christina Dunn   44
          Cara McKeating   45
          Laura Fitzsimons   46
          Lucy Williams   46
          Caoimhe McKeating   47
          Aoife Magee   47
          Áine Garland   48
          Fiona Brannigan   48
          Anna O'Hare   49
          Hannah Stratton   50
          Samantha Toman   50
          Aoife McMullan   51
          Vicky McCabe   51
          Louise Adams   52
          Emma Smyth   52

Dromore Central Primary School

Leia Marks	52
Laura McCandless	53
Andrew Cairns	54
Lauren Wallace	55
Jessica Magowan	55
Susannah Scott	56
Gareth Gribbon	56
Melissa Erwin	57
Claire McDonald	57
Melissa Hamilton	58
Jacqueline Gill	59
Johnny McMurray	59
Karen Campbell	60
Amy McNaugher	60
Gillian Poots	61
Kylie Skelton	61
Carolyn Black	62
Kirsty Wallace	62
Laura Poots	63
Hannah Chittick	64
Gillian Lowry	64
Gary Elliott	65
Claire Black	65
Adam Williamson	66
Harry McCorkell	66
Neil Aiken	67

Edenvale Primary School

Ryan McKnight	67
Rachel Ervine	68
Mark Anderson	68
Grace Frazer	69
Rachel Stewart	69
Kathryn Cromie	70
David Cromie	70

Grange Park Primary School

Richard Kavanagh	71
Julie Hanson	71
Kayleigh Richardson	72
Lorna Montgomery	72
James Farnham	73
Tom O'Hara	73
Naomi Pollock	74

Kilmaine Primary School

Joanne Chestnutt	74
Jenni Brittain	75
Kerry Watton	76
Erin Leslie Todd	76
Rachael Brady	77

Kirkistown Primary School

Andrew Bingham	77
James Douglas	78
Jolene Palmer	78
Emma Anderson	79
Tanith-Yola Finegan	80
Ryan Maginnes	80
Victoria Adair	81
Gareth Graham	81
Alison Brown	82
Rebecca Peden	82
Steven Evans	83
Zoe Adair	83
Brian Cromie	84
George Edward Calvert	84

Milltown Primary School

Emma Johnston	85
Graham Woods	85
Michelle Crangle	86
Eunice Dunlop	86

Portaferry Integrated Primary School

Hannah McGookin	87
Andrew McDowell	88
Peter Savage	88
Jervais Ashmore	89
James Reid	89
Zoe Gilmore	90
Hugh Mathews	90
Jonathan Reid	91
Andrew McCluskey	91
Charlene Ott	92
Mary-Jo Ellison	92

Poyntzpass Primary School

Rebecca Best	93
Colin Reaney	93
James Hammond	94
Neil Liggett	94
Debbie Long	95

Redburn Primary School

Steven Boal	96
Luke Somerville	96
Adam Makhfoudi	97
David Moore	97
Rachael Walker	98
Charlene Mallett	98
John Stephenson	99
Terri Reid	100
Jonathan Entwistle	100
Stuart Botham	101
Mary-Jayne Goodwin	101
Victoria Vine	102

St Brigid's Primary School, Newry

Clare O'Callaghan	102
Stephen Campbell	103
Aidan Garvey	103

Daniel Garvey   104
Amy Bradley   104
Ladean Rowland   105
Donna Reel   105
Evanna Kieran   106
Lisa Walsh   106
Carla McShane   106
Katie Harvey   107
Caoimhe Murphy   107
Thomas Walsh   108

St Clare's Primary School, Newry
Claire Heatley   108
Deirbhile Murphy   109
Shauna McParland   109
Natasha Kearns   110
Margaret Lisa Ward   110
Clare Rafferty   111
Claire McMurray   111

St Colman's Primary School, Moira
Nicole Doran   111
Danielle Mallon   112
Caroline McArdle   112
Jennifer Hull   113

St John's Primary School, Hillsborough
Keith Forsythe   113
Victoria Brown   114
Natalie Brown   114
Jonathan Walker   115
Nevin Spence   115
Christopher Walker   116
Emily Kennedy   116
Abigail Allen   117
Amy Oliver   118
Ruth Megarry   118
Andrew Simpson   119

Judith Caldwell   120
Samuel Ward   120

St Joseph's Primary School, Crossgar
        Karanne McCartan   121
        Caoimhe McErlane   122
        Nicole Lynch   122
        Mark Bell   123
        Thomas Ward   123
        Anna McKeown   124
        Lauren Casement   124
        Kevin Bell   125
        Conor McCartan   126
        Claire McCartan   127

St Joseph's Primary School, Downpatrick
        Carole Trueman   128
        Lynn Colhoun   128
        Leanne Murray   129
        Colette Lowry   129
        Nolene Trainor   130
        Orlaith Killen   130
        Hannah Lucas   131

St Joseph's Primary School, Killough
        Emma Lavery   131
        Aodhan Fitzsimmons   132
        Adam Holmes   132
        Sinead Burns   133
        David Hackett   133
        Natalie McGowan   134
        Shirley Briggs   134
        Nicola Laird   135
        Kieran Burns   136
        Laura Braniff   137
        Stephen Black   137
        Rachel Sharvin   138
        Cunliffe Fitzsimmons   139

Grainne Cupples   140
Oonagh Kelly   141
Brady Magee   141
Aoifa McEvoy   142

St Laurence O'Toole's Primary School, Newry
Nicola O'Callaghan   142
John Savage   143
Louise Helen Smith   144
Caoimhe Quinn   144
Jenny Rafferty   145
Dane Hayes   145
Rachel Rafferty   146
Nishia Hayes   146
Shane O'Hare   147
John Hearty   147
Kelly-Marie Smith   148

St Mary's Primary School, Banbridge
Darragh McCambridge   148
Kerri Winters   149
Paul Downey   149
Kris McGrath   150
Lucy Hillen   150
Lochlainn Hill   151
Tara Purdy   151
Daniel Smith   152
Conor Maginn   152
Sarah Murphy   153
Taylor Kearney   153
Caroline McCusker   154
John Kearns   154
Mark Pearce   155
Connor Quinn   155
Ciara Dunleavy   155
Gareth Smith   156
Áine Donnelly   156
Francesca McQuaid   156

Sarah McClean 157
Oisín Martin 157
Bronagh Campbell 158
Stephen Downey 159
Shane Nelson 159
Catherine Cunningham 160
Gary Buchanan 160
Corinne Jordan 161
Dana Kane 161
James Doran 162
Ruth Mulvenna 163
Carla McArdle 163
Andrew Lavery 164
Anna McArdle 164
Stephen Hynes 165

St Mary's Primary School, Killyleagh
Emma Boyle 166
Paul Woodside 166
Jacqlin Brown 167
David Gregge 167
Kirsty Nelson 168
Adele Gribben 168
Steven Fegan 169
Louise McGreevy 169
Kirsty Coughlin 169
Kathryn Clark 170
Gary Morrison 170
Connor Quinn 170
Danielle Doyle 171
Lori Cheevers 171
John Higgins 172
Nadine Corrin 173
Ashleen Carson 174
Shane Adair 174
Danielle Nelson 175
Vicky Bennett 175
Dean McComb 176

Sorcha Walsh   176
Caroline Walker   177
Joanne Sullivan   177
Claire Keenan   178
Michael Gregge   178
Matthew Nelson   179
Luke Turley   180
Ryan Stavely   181
Stacey Woodside   181
Antoinette Quinn   182
Anneka Perry   182
Christina Woodside   183

St Mary's Primary School, Kircubbin
Therese McGee   183
Therese Hoeritzauer   184
Andrew Ritchie   184
Tony Bowman   185
Kathryn McNamara   185
Conor Woods   186
Sarah Taylor   186
Shona Killen   187
Eugene Gilmore   188
Clare Quinn   188
Philip McMaster   189
Cheryl Masterson   189
Mark Morrison   190
Sarah Torney   190
Joanne Kelly   191
Conor Busuttil   191
Neill Caughey   192
Kerry Finnegan   193
Ross Torney   193
Cheryl Clarke   194
Christina Murray   194
Danny Fowler   195
Jonathan Dougherty   195
Sean Ennis   196

Gareth Finnegan   196
Julie McGrattan   197
Cathy Coyle   197

St Patrick's Ballygalget, Portaferry
Stephanie Flynn   198
Erin Healy   198
Lawrence Smyth   199
Vincent Toner   199
Michael Brennan   200
Aidan McKeating   200
Marie-Therese Coffey   201
Mary-Bridget Murray   201
Paul Keith   202
T P Harte   202

St Patrick's Boys' Primary School, Downpatrick
Gerard Collins   203
Daniel Mageean   203
Neil Morgan   204
Darryl Mason   204
Michael McCrissican   205
Rónán Kernan   206
Mark Magee   206
Mark Slavin   207
Philip Annett   208
Brian Scott   209

St Patrick's Primary School, Ballynahinch
Kieran Murphy   209
Darren Trimby   210
Maeve McCauley   210
Julie Murray   211
Rebecca McCann   211
Cormac Judge   212
Gregory Bonner   212
Louise Rooney   213
Stephanie Jones   213

Sinéad Marmion   214
Rebecca Smyth   214
Gerard Higgins   215
Clare Higgins   216
Christopher Rice   217
Natasha O'Connor   218
Caroline Davey   218
Christopher Molloy   219
Gerard O'Hare   220
Tammy Quinn   220
Victoria Noade   221

St Patrick's Primary School, Newry
Conor Nugent   221
Matthew Carberry   222
Ryan Conlon   222
Sean Evans   223
Danielle Brennan   223
Jade Teelan   223
Hannah Green   224
Karen Hanratty   224
Leanne Rushe   225
Ciara Rushe   225
Gary Harte   225
Leona Quinn   226
Keelan Conlon   226
Aveen Donaldson   227
Aoife Boyle   227
Geraldine Hearty   227

St Ronan's Primary School, Newry
Claire Toner   228
Conall Starrs   228
Emiear McShane   229
Emma Strain   229
Gavin Donald   230
Ronan Hughes   230
Shenna Matthews   231

Owen O'Donnell   232
Stephen McStay   232
Ciaran Fox   233
Conor Daly   233
Jonathan Philpott   234
Simon Hollywood   235
Fiona Flynn   235
Cathy Cassidy   236
Cliona Kane   236
Sarah Tumilty   237
Christopher Cunningham   237
James Patterson   238
Paula Gribben   238
Paul Burns   239
Lisa Burns   239
Ruth Quinn   240
Niall Boyle   240
Colleen Breen   241
Shane Barr   241
Claire Hegarty   242
Ruairi Digney   243
Naomi Boyce   243
Tara McGovern   244
John McCabe   244
Ross Mathers   245

West Winds Primary School
Narayan Kirk   245
Lauren Doole   246
Rachael Crawford   246
Kylie Martin   247

Windsor Hill Primary School
Chloe Miller   248
Karen Butler   248
Matthew McDowell   249

Haroula Pasparaki 249
Jonathan Tate 250
Iain McMillan 250

The Poems

WINTER

Meandering snowflakes
Freezing water
Slippery roads
Ice in gutter.

Slushy slush
Snow falling
Everyone look-out
Winter's calling.

Winter's gone
No more frost
Everyone say wahay!
Winter's lost.

Andrew Bell (9)
Andrews Memorial Primary School

HORSES

Horses are lovely
I like horses in every way
They are good to cuddle
They graze about in the field
Suzanne and I play with her pony.

I like jumping jumps
I like everything about horses
Horses are fun if you do anything
Suzanne's horse is called Hop.

Lorna McGrady (9)
Andrews Memorial Primary School

RABBITS

Rabbits have a lot of habits.
Hopping up and down around the town.
Eating grass and carrots.
Sleeping in hay.
Even peeping at bay.
Their fur coats are soft to touch.
They stay in a hutch or pen.
That is their den.

Amber Davis (9)
Andrews Memorial Primary School

SPACE

Up there in the night sky.
Somewhere beyond our reach
Is something quite extraordinary.

The only thing I would not like,
Is having no air to breathe!

Kristofer Best (9)
Andrews Memorial Primary School

HORSES

I think horses are adorable
They're gorgeous and cuddly
But some don't move at all
Some move swiftly
But most of all
I love horses!

Suzanne Majury (9)
Andrews Memorial Primary School

DINOSAURS DINOSAURS

Dinosaurs, dinosaurs, what do they eat?
Some eat plants and some eat meat.

Dinosaurs, dinosaurs, what do they do?
Some walk about and chase you.

Dinosaurs, dinosaurs, were they used for pets?
Or were they caught in fishing nets?

Dinosaurs, dinosaurs, where did you go?
Did you die in an explosion, or die in the snow?

Marc Wilson (9)
Andrews Memorial Primary School

BEANIES

Beanies appeal to all ages
Ages big or small
Animals that can be put in cages
Some that can't be at all

But Beanies are cute and cuddly
So I don't really care
What other people are thinking suddenly
So beware!

Victoria Brown (9)
Andrews Memorial Primary School

FOOTBALL

Football is the best
It is my favourite sport
I play every day
With my friends
I kick the ball to heaven
And to outer space.

The teams are so brilliant
That I watch them every day
It is so much fun
It's as good as a bun!
With a cherry on the top
I love football.

Ryan Galway (9)
Andrews Memorial Primary School

MY PONY

I have a pony
His name is Brandy
He is chestnut brown in colour
Brandy is fun to ride

Brandy grazes in the field
He hasn't a care in the world
Every night I bring him in
So he's safe and warm in his own home.

Jane Bicker (9)
Andrews Memorial Primary School

BEANIES

Beanies of all sizes,
Beanies all different colours.
They may even win prizes,
Some sisters, some brothers.

Some cats
Some dogs
Sit them on mats
But not on logs.

Lauren Alexander (9)
Andrews Memorial Primary School

SPORT

Sport is fun
Sport is fast
You can jump, skate and run,
I like sport.

Sport is rough and tough
Sport is speedy
I think I've had enough!
But I still like sport.

Gareth Eynon (9)
Andrews Memorial Primary School

FURBIES

I have a Furby
It is grey, white with stripes of blue
It is very funny
The material is stuck with glue
I must say it's like a bunny
I like my Furby
He has brown eyes
With a tongue and nose with ears
It can't play eye spy
Well not yet
I will never give it away
It is good to play with on rainy days.

Michelle Victoria Coey (9)
Andrews Memorial Primary School

BEES

Bees are very busy things
They buzz around all day
After they collect pollen for the hive
They go out and play
I don't really understand them
You probably don't understand them too
All I know is that they are very busy
But not half as busy as you.

Alison Fulford (9)
Andrews Memorial Primary School

TREES

Yellow branches
Leafless trees
Heavy sand
I love trees.
Leaves are yellow
Leaves are brown
Leaves go red in the
Autumn time.
Leaves are green
Leaves are dark
I like trees because
They have bark.

Ryan Connolly (9)
Andrews Memorial Primary School

BIRDS

Birds fly high in the sky
Soaring over treetops
Beaks glinting in the sun
Others perched on roofs.

Some on grassy lawns.
The crow with the worm in its beak
Ducks are by the pond
Their young ones in the nest.

Rachel Scott (9)
Andrews Memorial Primary School

TWO DAYS OUT

My girlfriend and I
Went to the sea.
We walked down the promenade
And she kissed me.
I felt so happy
I felt full of shock.
I nearly fell in the water
I nearly fell off the dock.

Then we went to the cinema
And watched a film or two,
Later on the next day
We went to the zoo.
And in the afternoon
We visited a mill.
But when I got home
Dad wasn't very happy
When I gave him the bill.

Graham Martin (11)
Andrews Memorial Primary School

FURBIES

Furbies are funny
But cost a lot of money
Furbies are sweet
And very neat
Furbies are nice to keep
They're quiet when they're asleep
I love Furbies.

Christopher McBride (9)
Andrews Memorial Primary School

STORMS

The electric wires hummed
Full of electricity
Rain drowned the city
Never going to end.

The people watched with horror
Out of their windows
While the birds took shelter
In their nests.

Then all of a sudden
The electric ended
It went dark
All through the town.

The storm went on
All through the night
But in the morning
The sun shone with delight!

Jenny Gouk (11)
Andrews Memorial Primary School

PRICES GO UP

I hate high prices
Especially petrol prices.
That's around twenty pounds.
When we go shopping
A packet of crisps
Are 90p. Some prices
Are cut down now.
Gratefully to say.

Caitlin Kirkwood (8)
Andrews Memorial Primary School

HEAVEN

Beautiful Calm
Loving Caring Relaxing
Bible Wings Dead Fire
Killing Burnings Depressing
Hell.

Allison Ferguson (11)
Andrews Memorial Primary School

SUMMER

Hot dry
Blazing shining welcoming
Sunlight snow ice
Freezing chilling isolating
Winter.

Jeanine Davidson (10)
Andrews Memorial Primary School

STRONG AND WEAK

Muscular, powerful
Strengthening, pulling, pushing
Weights, machines, feathers, joints
Weakening, sleeping, fainting
Weak.

Cara McDonald (11)
Andrews Memorial Primary School

IT ISN'T FAIR

It isn't fair, my room is bare
My mum gave all my toys away.
It isn't fair the sweet shop's
Gone - it was bombed.
It isn't fair my brother ate
The last pear and I am really
Starving!

It isn't fair my dad has
No hair and all my friends
Are laughing.
It isn't fair my brother shaved
My hair and blamed it all on
Me.
It isn't fair I'm really muddy
But . . . my mum is definitely
Not laughing.

Stuart Maguire (10)
Andrews Memorial Primary School

HEAVEN TO HELL

White, graceful
Loving, caring, forgiving,
Day calm, night noise
Daring, threatening, challenging
Hell.

Victoria Savage (10)
Andrews Memorial Primary School

FOOTBALL

First I played defence
And then goalkeeper
Now I play sweeper.

The goalie saves a shot
And carefully picks up the ball
He bounces the ball out
And passes to me
And I boot the ball up the field.

Then the right wing gets the ball
Going down the wing
He skins five and just passes the sixth,
Looking for someone in the box.

He crosses the ball
It goes higher and higher
To the back post
And a header by me means a
Goal!

Christopher Napier (11)
Andrews Memorial Primary School

FIRE

Flaming, hot,
Scalding, burning, roasting,
Ashes, flames, water, liquid,
Freezing, cooling, chilling,
Ice.

Glenn McKibbin (11)
Andrews Memorial Primary School

THE GNASH BIRD

The Gnash Bird is a creature rare,
But what an awesome sight!
And those who tangle with this bird
Age ten years overnight.

Its plumage is as black as coal -
The beak with teeth abounds;
And what a voice - it's louder than
A thousand, snarling hounds!

This flier builds a nest, of course,
In tree or house or spire.
But don't try pinching any eggs -
It's all made of barbed wire!

The Gnash Bird spreads its wings for flight
And then takes off - *Whoosh! Zoom!*
Best cover up your ears against
The supersonic *boom!*

For grub this bird scoffs anything -
A school - walls, roof and rafters,
Or dustbins by the tonne and then
An army tank for afters!

There isn't really such a bird -
Ignore what you've just read!
The whole Gnash Bird thing was made up
By the imagination in my head!

Rory Gibson (9)
Andrews Memorial Primary School

MY DOG

I have a little dog called Fido
His tummy just seems to get wider and
Wider.

His hair is all matted and long
And whenever he walks by
There's always a pong!

Wherever he is there's always a
Bad smell, everyone holds their noses
As well!

So as you can guess we were really
Embarrassed. So we sent him on a trip
All the way to Paris!

To a dog grooming parlour where he
Got bathed and groomed twice
And after that he did smell nice!

Sarah Hunter (10)
Andrews Memorial Primary School

THE THINGS WE SAW

You'll never guess what we saw
On our way to school
An old drunken man
Looking for the swimming pool.

We walked past our local shop
And a lady said to us
Oh, what lovely lassies
. . . . Why aren't you on the bus?

We walked past our friend's house
She ran out the door shouting wait wait!
It was so funny because
She was covered in paint.

We finally got to school
And met our other friends
We fell out with 'Paint Face'
But then we made amends.

Lynsey Gillespie (10)
Andrews Memorial Primary School

IT ISN'T FAIR!

When my brother made a mess
And tore my mum's dress
He blamed it on me
And I got no tea.

It isn't fair!
My mum caught me pulling my sister's hair
'But she started it!' I said
But she just put me to bed.

It isn't fair!
When my cousin went to the fair
My mum didn't take me
Because I didn't eat my tea.

Stephen McBurney (10)
Andrews Memorial Primary School

MY FAMILY

My mother can be pretty annoying,
All she ever says is,
'Do this. Tidy that room!'
Well, that's my mum.

My dad is nearly as bad,
He won't let you do anything mad
Apart from making swings in the tree
Well, that's my dad.

My brother is three times worse
He always has to get money
From my mum's purse,
And at 'homework time',
He always has to phone someone up,
Well, that's my brother.

My other brother is nicer
He always understands me
It is a real pity he's away,
In University. But I'll survive.

Help!

Claire Caldwell 11)
Andrews Memorial Primary School

SNOW

It is a really snowy day,
So we go out to play,
In the snow we go,
Our mothers always know.
Because we leave footprints in the snow,
And that is how they know.

Sam Long (11)
Andrews Memorial Primary School

MILLENNIUM BUG

The Millennium Bug has swept the Earth,
Bringing the computers to a new birth,
Starting them up, then breaking them down,
The Millennium Bug is all around.

If you start your computer up,
It may break down at twelve o'clock,
But if our experts are very quick,
They could maybe get it fixed.

The Millennium Bug walks through the towns,
Looking for places he hasn't yet found,
If he creeps into your house,
Call the experts to get him out!

Stephen Robinson (11)
Ballyholme Primary School

THE TREE

As I shed my leaves for the
Last time in this millennium
I wonder what the world will turn
Out like in the coming millennium.
I often think about this Millennium Bug
That I heard a couple of people chanting
About. That travels from house to house like
A ghost causing electrical problems. As a
Tree the only bug that I want is birds that
Nest on my branches. In the spring of 2000
I can't wait to display my new coat of
Leaves and blossoms and to hear the dawn
Chorus of the birds.
I look forward to being swayed into the new
Millennium as the winds of change blow.

Adhamh Callan-Rushe (11)
Ballyholme Primary School

MY SCHOOL

Ballyholme is the place to be,
Artistic talents are set free,
Learning subjects is made fun,
Laughing and joking, sharing a pun,
Yelling children skip and run,
Hockey, athletics, oh what fun!
Orchestras and choirs we have in our school
Lots of music we make, that's way cool!
Mr P is my teacher in P7,
Even English, maths and science are absolute
                                        heaven!

Louise Cochrane (11)
Ballyholme Primary School

MY LITTLE BROTHER

Eyes of blue, three foot two,
Curly hair upon his head.
Face like an angel
Calm and serene,
But deep inside
There's a devilish fiend.
He smiles as he nips you,
Grins when he kicks,
Laughs when he's up to
One of his tricks.
But as he sits there playing with toys
Thinking of one of life's many joys.
He is that angel
Calm and serene.
I wouldn't
Change him
Not one bit.
This wonderful being
My brother . . . . Tom

Jenni McClelland (11)
Ballyholme Primary School

BATS!

B ats are their name.
A erobatics is their game.
T actics they do best.
S ometimes they need a rest!

Danial Parker (11)
Ballyholme Primary School

A POEM ABOUT BATS!

B ats are blind,
A lthough they're caring and kind,
T hey come out at night,
S o they hide in the belfry at dawn's early light.

I t may seem strange that,
N ight's when they play.

T hey stay in the belfry,
H iding all day,
E nd of the day they go out for a fly.

B olting across the moonlit sky,
E nding the night,
L eaving their flight,
F atigued is he now, as he,
R ests upside down, so,
Y ou shouldn't be shocked if they're in your part of town!

David Thompson (11)
Ballyholme Primary School

BOYZONE

Boyzone, Boyzone an Irish pop group
They came into the world to make the girls look.
    They are the *best* singers, dancers and even cute
But Stephen makes me go mute.
    I have all their singles and albums too
I listen to them when I'm feeling blue.
    So if you want to brighten up your day
Shout *Boyzone! Boyzone!* Hip Hip Hooray !!!!

Kirsty Mulholland (10)
Ballyholme Primary School

An Alternative Alphabet

A stronomy studies the stars
B oxers will improve their skills
C omputers will become more up to date
D inosaurs are extinct
E verlasting memories we will still have
F orget the bad times
G et ready for a brand new start
H ave a great time in 1999
I f you are excited you will
J ust have to wait until the year 2000
K nowledge will increase
L ots of people will be waiting to wish each other a
      Happy New Year
M any astronauts may reach Mars
N obody knows what will happen
O n the year 2000 a plane will be flying at 12 o'clock
P eople may die nobody knows
Q ueen Elizabeth may step down from her reign
R ight at 12 o'clock many things will break down
S cientists will find out more information
T he millennium is very
U nusual as it happens only every 1000 years
V ikings will be forgotten
W orried people are all around
eX aminations are being done to make sure everything will be OK
Y o yo's were the toys for this year
Z ebra crossings help people to get across the street, hopefully
      many more good things will happen in the next *millennium.*

Lauren Morales (11)
Ballyholme Primary School

THE BEGINNING

The first day has come,
In a glittering sunrise,
The streets are bathed in liquid gold,
With no one in sight,
No one to enjoy this happy moment,
The sun rises, a glorious picture,
The millennium has begun.

Still people sleep on,
Far into the day,
While the party remains sit still,
And the sun blazes down,
Only to fall, fall down into the blue.
People stand watching the first day disappear.

Amy Finch (10)
Ballyholme Primary School

MILLENNIUM

Everyone is getting prepared,
Or at least, that is what I've heard.
They're panic-buying and storing up,
On all their goodies and bottles of pop.

The millennium is almost here.
So it's time to get some trendy gear.
We'll party on throughout the night.
The year 2000 is now in sight.

It may be dry or may be wet,
But it will be a day we'll never forget
Friday 31st December,
Is surely a date that we'll always remember.

Peter Irwin (11)
Ballyholme Primary School

CELEBRATION OR SORROW

The millennium, millennium. What do you think it'll bring?
Does pain and sorrow come with it, or joy and cause to sing?
That's what I am wondering when I lie awake in bed
And all those people in Africa. Are they being fed?

I know that people round the world are trying very hard.
To put things right that have been wrong. Not fiction, like Cpt Picard
But real people who are trying to save rainforests, once strong and tall
From people who for money, illegally make trees fall.

So that is what I think, of the world in which we live
And I'm glad to see some people not just receive but give.
They give to people they can see who really need them most
And I am glad that they do that, and none of them boast.

Lauren Cheshire (9)
Ballyholme Primary School

MILLENNIUM

What's going to happen
When it comes?
Will we be affected
By the Millennium Bug?
The year 2000
Everyone's excited
What's going to happen?
Will the Earth stop turning?
Will the sun stop burning?
Nobody knows,
What's going to happen?

Sarah Leinster (11)
Ballyholme Primary School

JACK FROST

As he slowly creeps under the doors of innocent people,
Freezing all whom he meets,
Animals, statues and trees.
People dread winter every day in case Jack Frost
                        wants to play!
It's like a big dark cloud has covered the earth,
And swallowed up all the colour.
People hope that spring hurries up and comes their way.
Jack Frost is only content when his icy path covers
                        the earth.
All the world shouts a plea,
'Could Jack Frost just leave us alone and come back
                        for another winter?'
When he leaves, all of them shout with glee,
'Hooray he has gone at last!'

Sarah Coghlan (11)
Ballyholme Primary School

MUM'S BIRTHDAY

Mum's birthday filled with joy
Springing into hearts
Never failing nor forgetting
Presents, food, cards.
Friends and family come
Lifting everyone's hearts
Bringing all the love she needs
To brighten her day
For a special Mother's treat.

Erin Mullan (11)
Ballyholme Primary School

FROST

Winter has come.
The wind will roar.
Frost is everywhere.
On an iced floor.

Frost is here.
And covers the land.
Little children.
With glove covered hand.

Iced cold patterns.
Freeze the puddles.
Children play.
In little huddles.

Then at night.
When we go in.
The frost will leave.
But come again.

Edward Hewitt (11)
Ballyholme Primary School

GREETINGS

Greetings fellow Earthlings,
I come to you in peace.
I have brought with me my golden crown,
Which I will show you in this town.
I have travelled here from space
To announce that I am King.
A King you may be surprised.
For I have come to see your
Queen!

Francesca Darrah (11)
Ballyholme Primary School

SCHOOL

The thought of school - it makes me sick
It's very sad - really wick'
Sitting in a chair all day
Do I want to be here - *no way!*

Maths and English, science too
All the things I hate to do
Work and study all the time
It's a shame! It's a crime!

Teachers nag over little things
Tie your hair back, remove those rings
Pull your socks up, roll down that skirt
Tie your laces and tuck in your shirt.

On the bus that's taking me home
I'm dreading the homework that has to be done
Hurry up weekend, at last I'll be free
No reading, no writing, *no teachers!*
                              Yippee!

Zara Gilroy (11)
Ballyholme Primary School

WAR IN IRELAND

War and peace will fight battles forever,
There may be peace and then it will sever.
Bone-strucken arguments rattle on,
What I wish for cheering and battle be gone.
So many deaths of innocent lives,
I plead for peace but no answer is replied.
What I ask for, peace, is not that much.
Peace, please, Peace!

Suzanna Clark (10)
Ballyholme Primary School

MILLENNIUM PARTY

New Year's Eve is coming
I'm ready for a party
I can hear what's going on
People happy and laughing.

New Year's Eve is closer
The amusement is arriving
The party food is popping
Everybody is excited.

New Year's Eve is here
We're singing 'Auld Lang Syne'
Everybody's partying
Has our world just changed?

Kerry Savage (10)
Ballyvester Primary School

LET'S PARTY

It's time to party
Hear the glasses go clank
It's time to party
Until our heads go blank

We're partying now
And we're having fun
We're partying now
Until the night is done

Hear the clock chime twelve
When everybody cheers
Hear the clock chime twelve
Happy New Year!

Leona Wells (10)
Ballyvester Primary School

MILLENNIUM PARTY YEAR

The millennium year brings lots of cheer
Party food sounds really good
Relations and friends it never ends
The millennium party year

Television, space, the human race
Up and down dancing around
Photos, snips and computer chips
The millennium party year.

We'll keep our smile party a while
Stay up all night to our delight
Jump to the left then to the right
Like I said we'll party all night.

Roxanne Aicken (10)
Ballyvester Primary School

MILLENNIUM

Millennium, millennium it's such a bore.
I don't understand,
I want to know more
I'd rather go sit in some sinking sand.

Millennium, millennium, what is it about?
They say 'Be quiet I'm catching a trout.'
I go away sad and very confused
I guess I'll just have to watch the news.

Jacqui Beattie (11)
Ballyvester Primary School

WHY SHOULD WE CELEBRATE THE MILLENNIUM?

Why should we celebrate the millennium?
It's just another night
After all in the 21st century
We've got lots of things to put right.

The world has come a long, long way
But with man polluting the air
The world will surely end some day
And it seems like no one cares.

Laurie Symon (11)
Ballyvester Primary School

YEAR 2000

The year 2000 will be great
On that night we will celebrate
Disco lights so much more
On that night it will be fun galore.

Some people may think a different way than me
I think the night will be great you see
Groove here, groove there
People dancing everywhere.

The year 2000 will be great
On that night we will celebrate.

Claire Breadon (11)
Ballyvester Primary School

2000

Let's celebrate the millennium
Let's celebrate 2000
But wait! Look at the world.

Can we go on the way we are with
War and disease everywhere.
The environment is like the Titanic
Sinking, never to be brought back to life.

Can we do anything to prevent it?
We need to get our acts together.
Stop talking about what we should do,
Let's get to work!

Let's turn it around and celebrate
The millennium, always remembering
To look at the world.

Ryan Lee (10)
Ballyvester Primary School

CELEBRATION 2000

When the year 2000 comes.
I'm going to party.
Everyone will wonder and dream
About what the future holds.

When the year 2000 comes.
I'm going to put up balloons and paper chains.
I'll welcome anyone who passes by
When the year 2000 comes.

Laura Gourley (10)
Ballyvester Primary School

THE WEATHER

When the sun is glistening in the sky
The birds are singing as they fly by

At night when the moon is shining
Around the Earth it leaves a golden lining

As lightning goes crashing day and night
There are little children in bed with a fright.

When the rain comes scampering down to Earth
The people will have to buy new turf

When the snow will be tingling down
The children will be playing within the town

When the hailstones and sleet come crashing on the roof
The dog will bark like this, woof woof

All this weather comes throughout the year
When we live in this country here.

Bronagh Clare Getty (9)
Cedar Integrated Primary School

TREE SPIRIT

The trees have fruits like grapes, oranges and cherries.
Some people say that the trees have fairies.
The people don't know how much love the spirits bring.
It's as soft and gentle as a piece of string.
The tree's spirit is a beautiful thing.
If you listen you might hear them sing.
The trees are huge and tall.
The roots are so tight that they don't fall.

Natalie Savage (9)
Cedar Integrated Primary School

IMAGINE

Imagine a world of peace
Wouldn't that be great.
With no fighting or bombing
We don't have to hate.

Imagine a world of peace
Wouldn't that be fun.
No maiming or killing
Throw away that gun.

Imagine a world of peace
Wouldn't that be good.
People in the third world
Would have drink and food.

Imagine a world of peace
Wouldn't that be fine.
One day it will happen
The decision is yours and mine.

Francesca Whaley (9)
Cedar Integrated Primary School

MY SPIRIT

My spirit flies above me
So high that it reaches the sky.
Through the clouds it speaks to me.
It says how it loves and how it cares.
Every night when I am in bed
I can hear it in my head.

Catherine Speers (8)
Cedar Integrated Primary School

DREAMS

Dreaming dreaming I could fly
Dreaming dreaming I could touch the sky
Dreaming dreaming I could fly a plane
Dreaming dreaming I could go to Spain

Dreaming dreaming I saw a dinosaur
Dreaming dreaming if only they were alive once more
Dreaming dreaming I swam with a whale
Dreaming dreaming I kissed a snail

Dreaming dreaming I was a frog
Dreaming dreaming I went for a jog
Dreaming dreaming I went to Jupiter
Dreaming dreaming I came back even stupider

Mark Kirk (9)
Cedar Integrated Primary School

PEACE IS FLOWING LIKE A RIVER

Peace is flowing
Peace is flowing like a river.
Flowing from you and me.
Spreading throughout this land.
To stop the gun in the gunman's hand.

Peace is flowing like a river.
Flowing from you and me.
Spreading throughout this land.
Make the politicians take a stand.

Caitlin Morrison (9)
Cedar Integrated Primary School

THE WORLD OF BOOKS

There are different kinds of books, big ones and small
One time I dreamt I was with them all!
First I was sliding down a long book
Which had a very odd look.
Then I went to my favourite part
To see the books I knew by heart.
But then I noticed all the books run
And I thought 'There goes the fun.'
'Goodbye, goodbye' said all the books
Running away with funny looks
Some were laughing some were sad
Some felt awful some felt glad.
Then I noticed I was in bed
'It must have been a dream' I said.

Emma Morgan (9)
Cedar Integrated Primary School

THE MOON

The moon shone down on you and I,
The lonely light lit up the sky.
The children lay upon their beds,
With moonlight shining on their heads.
The moonlight shone on stormy seas,
Deserted fields and tall pine trees.
All was dark and still that night,
Only the moon was shining bright.

Stephen Cullum (9)
Cedar Integrated Primary School

DAN'S SNOWMAN

Dan built a snowman one day
And put a scarf on to keep the cold away
With buttons for his eyes
A carrot for his nose
A big round belly
But forgot to give him toes
He gave him a hat and a stick
And said that should do the trick.

Andrew Spence (9)
Cedar Integrated Primary School

SNOW

Look at the snow
See all the different drops.
When it falls you build snowmen.
Oh. It is so nice.

Look at the snow.
The snow comes falling down.
Pitter-patter, pitter-pitter,
The snow comes falling down.

Pitter-patter snowdrops
Look at the lovely snowdrops.
Pitter-patter snowdrops.
The snowdrops come falling down.

Carrie Anne Crolly-Burton (9)
Convent of Mercy Primary School

I KNOW A CAT

I know a cat
Who is fluffy
And cheeky
It sits
On your lap
And then
Drives you crazy

I know a cat
Who chases
Its tail
And then
When it
Gets it
It does
It again.

Emma Stranney (11)
Convent of Mercy Primary School

MY DOG

My dog is black and white
My dog has a wriggly tail
My dog is called Tinker.

Every day I take Tinker for a walk.
I feed Tinker every day.
I love my dog so much.

I bath him every Sunday
He does not like baths
My dog can do lots of tricks.

Clara Keenan (9)
Convent of Mercy Primary School

CATS

I love cats,
Especially Postman Pat's
I love fluffy cats
They're nothing like rats
I love kittens
With fluffy mittens
I love kittens sweet and kind
They are not very hard to find
I love the cat that chases the mouse
Because it keeps him out of the house
I hate the ones that bite
They give me such a fright
I love the ones with silky fur
I also love it when they purr.

Janine McGrady (11)
Convent of Mercy Primary School

EGGS

Runny, drippy, squishy eggs
Covered in potatoes and
Mayonnaise.
Yellow on the inside and
White round the edge.
Dive your chips in the
Mayonnaise.
When you've done that take
A bit - then I think you
Might just quit.
And that is all about eggs.

Sarah Rice (10)
Convent of Mercy Primary School

THE WITCH

She comes out at night,
On her broomstick, she flies
Over us.
In front of our eyes
Her ugly face.
With her crooked teeth,
Warts all over her,
With her little black cat.
Her cauldron bubbles
With poison inside
And all gruesome things
That you find outside.
She has lots of fun,
But then before dawn,
She goes back in
With a long horrible
Y a w n!

Catherine Dougherty (10)
Convent of Mercy Primary School

MY SISTER

Once in my bed
I looked down and said
To my sister below
'If you'd like to know,
I have to say
This very day
You're the best sister
I ever had.'

Maria O'Hare (11)
Convent of Mercy Primary School

THE NEW HOUSE

The new house is a good house
It is a very good house.
With a lot of space.
Space, space, space!
Big windows,
Big doors,
Big floors,
Big rooms,
The new house is a good house
And we're moving in
                    soon!

Grainne Teggart (10)
Convent of Mercy Primary School

SALAD

Salad is so good for you,
It makes you feel new.
If you look closely,
You will see,
Lettuce,
Tomatoes,
Eggs
And celery,
Celery, celery!

Daena Walker (11)
Convent of Mercy Primary School

THE WALK

I went for a walk
Under the trees swaying
With no one to talk to
Just the sound of the donkey braying

Down the lane, over the hill
Past the river, through the gate
And there I saw a man stood still
Who said he was ever so late
To go on a date

Homeward bound to get my tea
Eyes heavy and feet sore
But ever so glad
To spend time with me.

Danielle McDowell (10)
Convent of Mercy Primary School

LOVE

Love is what you've got to give
It will never fade
Share it with that special someone
Do not be afraid

Love is what you've got to give
For your mum and dad
Love is everything you need
Love is what you'll always have

Julie-Ann Rodgers (11)
Convent of Mercy Primary School

THE STARS

The stars are very beautiful
Especially at night
They wink and blink at me
They glitter and sparkle at night
I wish they wouldn't go away
But I know if they won't go away
Then I may not see the light of day.

Kathleen Ward (11)
Convent of Mercy Primary School

MY BABY BROTHER

My baby brother is ten months old
He's got 2 teeth.
And he is very bald
He cries all night and sleeps all day
He claps his hands and runs away.

Sarah McAuley (10)
Convent of Mercy Primary School

THE MOON

The moon is like
A ball of cheese
I wish I could
Have a piece
Of that yummy!
Yummy! Cheese.

Michelle Murray (11)
Convent of Mercy Primary School

THE BUNNY RABBIT

It hops, silently, through the woods
So silently,
The way it should,
No trace of paw or mark.
Looking for food here and there
But I don't think there's food anywhere
The people come to knock down trees
The rabbit's sad when its home leaves,
So I take it home,
My head's in a muddle,
I'm sure this will get me into big trouble.
I knock on our door, my mum comes out
She says 'Laura, what's all this about?'
With a hop and a skip
Bunny is out of my arms
Heading for the bushes
Now what's the harm?

Laura Polly (10)
Convent of Mercy Primary School

MY CAT

Pittery pat
Goes my cat.
Early in the morning,
Gorging her food.
How very rude!
Early in the morning
I think she snores
But never roars
Early in the morning, morning, morning . . .

Rebecca Gribben (11)
Convent of Mercy Primary School

MR AND MRS DUKELOW

Katrina spied Victor four years ago,
In fact they met through work.
When Katrina saw Victor Dukelow,
She nearly went berserk.
An eligible bachelor he seemed to be,
To wed him that was her intention
So their romance began in earnest,
And they promised us a day to remember,
And told us all,
The date was set for September
Two years later in December
Katrina, Victor and little James!

Lisa Totten (11)
Convent of Mercy Primary School

FAMILY

Family is who you've got,
To love and care for you,
You should respect them a lot.

They care for you when you're
Sick or feeling down,
You should respect them a lot.

They are there for you,
When you've got no one else,
You should respect them a lot.

Nathanya McColl (11)
Convent of Mercy Primary School

THE MILLENNIUM BUG

This Millennium Bug is causing concern.
But how it works we soon will learn.
Tall or small bugs, we don't know.
Come 2000 it's sure to show.

Some say it will affect our life.
Bringing havoc, and causing strife.
Electric, gas and water confused,
We won't have any money to use.

They plan to celebrate with cheer,
Bringing in the Millennium New Year.
They even built a Millennium Dome,
I think it's for the Bug's new home.

Ciara Vance (11)
Convent of Mercy Primary School

THE STARS

I have always wondered
What are stars,
Why are they only out at night?
Maybe because of the moonlight
Are they big or are they small?

That is what I want to know,
Some people say 'They are big'
Some people say 'They are small'
But - all I want to know is
Are they big or are they small?

Christina Dunn (9)
Convent of Mercy Primary School

THE RACE

Cleaning goggles,
Pulling down your cap,
Up on the diving block,
All in a flap.

Ready for the whistle,
There it goes,
Through the air,
With pointed toes.

Into the water,
Swimming underneath,
Break the surface,
Gritting your teeth.

Legs kicking hard,
Arms pulling with all their might,
Turning and gliding
Ready to put up a fight.

Back up the pool
Nearly done,
Into the lead,
Yes . . . I've won!

Cara McKeating (11)
Convent of Mercy Primary School

THE ALIEN FROM MARS WHO CATCHES STARS

The man from Mars
He catches stars.
And even eats them with chocolate bars.
He catches cod,
With his fishing rod
And gives them to his cat called Mod,
The man from Mars is very green.

He's the funniest man I've ever seen.
I've seen him catch stars.
And eat them with chocolate bars.
I've seen him catch cod,
And give it to his cat called Mod.
The man from Mars is very green,
It's the funniest thing I've ever seen.

Laura Fitzsimons (9)
Convent of Mercy Primary School

THE LITTLE FIR TREE

The little fir tree stood alone,
        With the ice and cold of the winter snow.
All the tall trees had gone away,
        To be Christmas trees in a house some day
The little fir gave a groan,
        'I wish I could be a Christmas tree in a home.'
Some years later it too got chopped down,
        And was soon the best Christmas tree in town.

Lucy Williams (9)
Convent of Mercy Primary School

SPRING

Here comes spring
Where the grass grows so green.
The flowers grow
Crocuses and primrose.
How lovely to see
The baby lambs being born
They jump and skip
And hop at dawn.

The sun shines,
All over the trees
They sway in the wind,
And swoosh in the breeze.
The birds chirp
In the blue sky
and the wind whistles
At sunrise.

Caoimhe McKeating (9)
Convent of Mercy Primary School

SCHOOL

How I just love to work and play,
And see all my friends every day,
How I just love schooldays in the sun,
It makes them oh so much fun.
How I love the school summer days,
But I hate the school winter days.
How I just love to work and play,
And see all my friends every day.

Aoife Magee (8)
Convent of Mercy Primary School

AUTUMN

Autumn is a wonder.
Leaves fall from the trees.
Winds howl in the night.
Birds stop singing in the trees.

Leaves make a blanket on the woodland floor
A kite flies by in the sky.
Birds are leaving the country to
Fly to warmer places.

Now you see people wearing hats
And scarves
The dog curls up in his kennel.
There are great storms in the sky.

Áine Garland (8)
Convent of Mercy Primary School

THE SEASONS

The seasons change day by day
And with the changes so does our play.
Spring is snowdrops and primroses
And baby lambs with their little black noses.
Summer we play hopscotch and skipping
And when the weather's fine we go for a dipping.
Autumn means red, orange, yellow and brown
Beautiful leaves now on the ground.
Winter brings us games inside
Certainly not days by the tide.
God's love shown to us in his seasons
Every one for different reasons.

Fiona Brannigan (9)
Convent of Mercy Primary School

WEATHER

The weather may blow,
The weather may snow,
The weather may be hot,
It may sizzle in a pot.

The weather may be warm,
Then we can go to the farm,
The weather may rain,
But it shan't give us pain.

I love it when the weather's sunny,
I hate it when the weather's rainy,
We have no fun,
When there is no sun.

The weather might be dull,
The weather might be bright,
We shall have fun,
Or we shall have a fight?

It may not snow,
And the flowers may grow,
We might have light,
When the sun shines so bright.

Anna O'Hare (9)
Convent of Mercy Primary School

WHEN I BROKE MY TOE

When I broke my toe
I got quite a shock you know.
I cried with pain
But got no gain.
Cos Mummy said I deserved it.

I was fighting with my brother
'Stop that!' said my mother.
I did not care
I kicked the chair,
But Mummy said I deserved it.

The doctor he examined it
And 'yes' there was a broken bit,
My toe was black
My shoe was slack.
Still Mummy said I deserved it.

Hannah Stratton (10)
Convent of Mercy Primary School

MY LITTLE BROTHER

My little brother gets on my nerves.
Mummy puts him to bed early, that's what
                                    he deserves.
He kicks, and he nips, and he bites.
And he always looks for fights.
But deep, deep down in my heart.
I love him and miss him when we are
                                    apart.

Samantha Toman (9)
Convent of Mercy Primary School

THE BIZZY BEE

Bizzy busy bumblebee
Bizzy bizzy bee

Busy looking for honey
Buzzing through the trees

Busy as a bee
Buzzing at the children with ice-cream
on their knees

That big yellow striped bee.

Aoife McMullan (9)
Convent of Mercy Primary School

OH NO!

Tricky Vicky is so bad;
When she's gone everyone's glad.
Happy happy all day long
Oh no
She's back
And ready for action
Knock knock
She's back.

Oh no!

Vicky McCabe (10)
Convent of Mercy Primary School

MY TOY

My toy is fluffy and white,
It is cuddly and sweet
I sleep with it between my feet,
His name is Lucky
He's my favourite teddy
I love him so much I
Could jump for joy.

Louise Adams (9)
Convent of Mercy Primary School

THE SKY

The sky is blue, beautiful blue
With stars like twinkling crystal.
The sun lies up in the beautiful sky
And so does the big white moon.
How could we live without the sky?
I don't know but I love it.

Emma Smyth (9)
Convent of Mercy Primary School

THE COLOUR BLUE

Blue is the sky on a hot summer's day.
Blue is rain pouring down.
Blue is a waterfall beside the bank,
Blue is the water I just drank.

Blue is my pen which ran out of ink.
Blue is a lake frozen all night,
Blue is the creatures of the ocean,
Blue is happiness all around.

Blue is the coldness on a winter's day
Blue is slippery, rainy and wet
Blue is happy but sometimes sad,
Blue is the jumper of my dad.

Blue is a beautiful colour that I love to
See.

Leia Marks (10)
Dromore Central Primary School

WHAT IS YELLOW?

Yellow reminds me of the sun
Shining high in the sky.
Yellow is a colour mixed with red
And orange in a fire.
Yellow is a lively colour
And comes dazzling from disco
lights.
Yellow is for the lovely sandy
Beaches when I'm on holiday,
Or the sunflowers blossoming
On a lovely summer's day.
Yellow is the colour of buttercups
Growing among the fresh green
grass.
When I see yellow
I think of a pot of gold
You would find at the end of a
rainbow.

Laura McCandless (11)
Dromore Central Primary School

LAMBCHOP DREAMING

Lambchop lay in a smelly bin,
He was old fat and bones,
Soon the cats would be in for him.

He didn't like to be this way,
He shut his eyes and dreamed back,

Back to when he was on the plate,
Steaming hot with mint sauce,
With turnip and cauliflower cheese,
A man with a knife and fork ready to eat him.

He didn't like to be this way,
He shut his eyes and dreamed back.

Back to when he was in the butcher shop,
Beside sausages and stewing meat,
Everybody shouting, 'Not me! Not me!'

He didn't like to be this way,
He shut his eyes and dreamed back.

Back to when he was in the abattoir,
Hung up beside cows and pigs,
Getting taken down and cut up,
Into lambchops and legs of lamb.

He didn't like to be this way,
He shut his eyes and dreamed back.

Back to when he was in the field,
Skipping with his friends,
Playing games and frolicking.

He liked to be this way,
He dreamed hard to try to stay there.

Andrew Cairns (10)
Dromore Central Primary School

A Snowy Day

Snow! Snow!
Thick, thick, snow.
Falling quietly to the ground
All the children yelling, shouting,
Very happy that the snow's around.
The roof is like a birthday cake,
Snowflakes falling on the lake,
Smooth and clean and frosty white
Gleaming, sparkling, through the night.
Children make snowmen all the day
And slide upon their slippery sleigh,
But then the thaw so quickly comes
And my poor fingers feel like thumbs.

Lauren Wallace (10)
Dromore Central Primary School

Loneliness

Loneliness is white,
It tastes like sour grapes
And smells like a dump.
It looks like an open place
But no one is there.
It sounds like nothing at all.
Loneliness feels like a cage
And I just want to
Scream!

Jessica Magowan (10)
Dromore Central Primary School

BLUE AS A BLUEBELL

Blue is a bluebell,
That has the sweetest smell.
A moon in the sky,
Like a blueberry pie!
A colour of the rainbow as you lie,
A magical bridge across the sky.
A winter blanket across the land,
But up above as blue as a ribbon band.
Blue has calmness, happiness and
Sadness.
And when you relax you'll have some
Gladness!

Susannah Scott (11)
Dromore Central Primary School

GREEN

Green is like freedom
The grass and the open fields.
Green is like jealousy.
Green is envy
When you don't get what you want.
Apples are a soft green.
Bananas are green
When they are not ripe.
Green smiles like
Freshly cut grass.
Green is nature.
Green is everywhere.

Gareth Gribbon (11)
Dromore Central Primary School

BLACK

Black is sadness,
Death and mourning.
Black is horror,
And pitch-black darkness.
Black is loneliness,
Like being left on your own.
And it reminds me of,
Horrible pollution in a big city.
Black are ashes,
From a burnt-out fire.
Smoke and dullness,
Horrible all around!

Melissa Erwin (11)
Dromore Central Primary School

BUMBLEBEE

I'm black and yellow
Sometimes I sting!
I make honey
From the plants
I see.
But people don't
Like
Me!

Claire McDonald (10)
Dromore Central Primary School

WHAT IS?

What is a lily,
Floating in a pond?
What is a lamb,
Running beyond?
What is the snowdrop,
The first sign of spring?
What is the blossom,
On a summer's tree?
What is a page,
In a school book?
What is the marshmallow,
Which the children took?
What is chalk dust,
On a blackboard?
What is a terrier,
Chewing on a cord?
What is a cloud,
On a summer's day?
What is fresh snow,
With children wanting to play?
What is loneliness,
In the playground?
What is this thing,
That surrounds us all around?

Melissa Hamilton (10)
Dromore Central Primary School

THE WONDROUS COLOUR GREEN

Green is an open field,
And trees that yield.
Green is the feeling of freedom,
Swaying in a fancy kingdom.
Green is so calm,
Comforting a lamb!
Green is the changing of leaves,
And blazes of grass in big sheaves.
Green is the colour that makes you
Queasy,
And sometimes the grass makes you
Sneezy!
Green is the colour of a palm tree,
Growing as tall as you can see!

Jacqueline Gill (11)
Dromore Central Primary School

PURE WHITE

White is a dove which flies high,
White is a cloud far up in the sky,
White is a snowman which will thaw,
White is a bandage for a dog's
Wounded paw,
White is a sheet on a very nice bed,
White is the heavens which pick up the
Dead,
White is the pages of the book I've read,
White are the things I've explained and
Said.

Johnny McMurray (11)
Dromore Central Primary School

RED

Red is a blazing fire, warm and
cosy,
Red is hot with anger inside
yourself,
Red is for tomatoes and blood,
Red is for love meaning a
relationship,
Red means to be disgraced,
Red is for Red Nose Day,
Red means to be bold,
Red can be the colour of autumn
leaves.

Karen Campbell (11)
Dromore Central Primary School

MILLENNIUM!

It's Jesus' birthday,
Two thousand today.
Hip hip hooray!
This is such a special date,
For which I can hardly wait.
It's time to celebrate!
Although He's very old,
His story still is told,
And He's worth more than gold!
He'll never change,
He'll stay the same,
Year in year out until the next
millennium!

Amy McNaugher (11)
Dromore Central Primary School

MILLENNIUM, MILLENNIUM

Millennium, millennium
You will be here soon.
Causing problems for computers
And airlines.
What will we do!
Some will be excited others just think
It is the same as any other year.
But it isn't, it is going to be a thrilling and
Interesting year.
Well I wonder do you know why?
Yes, it is Christ's 2000 birthday.
Whooh, what a long, long time to live.
But most of all we know nobody will live to
2000 years old.
No way!
This is what the millennium is about,
Christ.

Gillian Poots (11)
Dromore Central Primary School

MILLENNIUM

M any people getting organised.
I llusions of what's to happen.
L ove and
L aughter
E verywhere,
N ations
N ear and far.
I   magining events of neighbouring friends.
U nable to control thoughts of the future
M illennium

Kylie Skelton (11)
Dromore Central Primary School

THE NEW MILLENNIUM

2000 years of life on Earth,
People making lots of fuss,
What could all this be worth,?
The next 2000 is up to us.
But you should all remember a special birthday,
The birthday of Jesus Christ.
This very spectacular date
Is something worth to celebrate.
He was the one whose Father created,
The sun, stars and moon
The giant elephant to the small racoon.
And last but not least man.
But fate fell upon the earth,
As man and woman committed a sin,
By eating a forbidden fruit,
And into their hearts Satan entered in.
But let us not worry
So we can celebrate
This special day,

Jesus' birthday!

Carolyn Black (11)
Dromore Central Primary School

MILLENNIUM

The Millennium Bug
Is trying to tug
Computers off their side.

The millennium is near
There is some fear
It's only one more year.

Only one more year to go
It is creeping very slow
Will electricity be a steady flow?
That's what everyone wants to know.

It's on its way
We all have to say,
Hip hip hooray!

Kirsty Wallace (11)
Dromore Central Primary School

ALWAYS REMEMBER

The year 2000 is nearly upon us,
And people around us are caught up in fuss,
Making plans for this big celebration,
Although panic and fear grip the nation.
Computers and electronics are causing
Confusion,
I wonder and ponder and drift into elusion,
People will celebrate in so many ways,
I hope they remember there's only 24 hours in a
Day.
There will be big money spent on parties galore,
And some will turn out to be quite a bore,
But I just wonder how I'll celebrate,
January 2000 that big date!
Many Christians will celebrate his birth,
All colours, all nations, throughout the Earth,
Others live in fear of his coming again,
But always remember God is in reign.

Laura Poots (11)
Dromore Central Primary School

MILLENNIUM

M is for the Millennium Bug. It is out to get computers.

I is for Into space. Some day we could do it too!

L is for the Lord Jesus Christ, who is celebrating His 2000thbirthday.

L is for let's celebrate to the future and Christ's birthday.

E is for electronic everything! Laptops, palm tops, fax machines too!

N is for never fear, for the millennium is near!

N is for needy people. You would think they were all gone by now!

I is for the Internet. The international way to communicate.

U is for the ultimate party experience!

M is for making peace. Isn't it about time?

Hannah Chittick (11)
Dromore Central Primary School

MILLENNIUM!

M any parties held tonight,

I n honour of the new millennium.

L isten to the church bells ring,

L ooking forward to what the new year brings.

E verywhere around the world people celebrate.

N ight sky's lit by candlelight,

N eighbours greet with delight.

I n peaceful joy we meet,

U nited in hope for the new,

M *illennium!*

Gillian Lowry (10)
Dromore Central Primary School

MILLENNIUM BUG PARTY

Inside every computer, little bugs lie in wait.
They don't know it there'll be a party,
The bug governors are still having a debate.
They dream about the millennium party,
Drinking wine and tea.
Playing lots of funny games,
Wrecking your PC!
So if it's the millennium,
And you hear lots of noise.
Turn on your PC.
Electrocute them, don't play with your toys.

Gary Elliott (11)
Dromore Central Primary School

MILLENNIUM

M illennium
I mproved technology
L aptops
L ate night parties
E nd of 1999
N ext 1000 years
N ationwide
I   t is Jesus' 2000th birthday
U niversal
M assive celebrations

Claire Black (11)
Dromore Central Primary School

THE MILLENNIUM PARTY

Loud music, screams and shouts,
What could it be?
Aaagh! I forgot,
It's the millennium!

I'm just in time
To see Big Ben
Bong, Bong, Bong, Bong, Woo Hoo!
The uproar comes
Join the millennium
Join the party.

Adam Williamson (11)
Dromore Central Primary School

DRAGONS

Dragons smell like a fishmonger's on a hot day.
Dragon's eyes are golden and its tail is like a whip.
Its skin is leather, its wings beat the night air.
Its claws are as sharp as daggers.
Some dragons are dangerous and some dragons are
Fun and all dragons are good.
Dragons, well . . .
All this is for dragons to know.
Dragons are the great story keepers of the world.

Harry McCorkell (10)
Dromore Central Primary School

WHAT IS GREEN?

Green is jealousy
And envy.
Green is the colour of slime
And the smell of sickness
Green is the freedom of
The countryside,
And trees and plant life
Which grow inside.
Green is the freshness
Of grapes and apples.

Neil Aiken (11)
Dromore Central Primary School

THE MILLENNIUM IS HERE!

The millennium will soon be here,
Just a few months to go.
January 1st 2000
The millennium is very near.

The Millennium Dome soon opens,
And I'll maybe be there,
I'll be there with Mum and Dad
And we'll maybe see the Mayor.

Ryan McKnight (11)
Edendale Primary School

NEW THINGS AROUND

I wonder what it will be like!
I wonder what is new!
Will there be different things around?
I think there will be different things too.

Go to the Dome in London,
And look at the new things around,
Walk about to see the sights,
And don't make a sound.

I think it will be grand to see
The wonderful, brilliant sight,
The Dome standing high in the sky,
Bright as can be in the millennium light.

Rachel Ervine (11)
Edendale Primary School

THE MILLENNIUM

The millennium we have fun,
When we run and sing,
When we go out and about.

The millennium will soon be here,
And it will be fun,
We are going to have a party,
And I hope there will be a lot of sun.

Mark Anderson (10)
Edendale Primary School

TIME TO PARTY

It's now time to party,
The 12 chimes are on,
And we will party
Right to dawn.

The Dome is going up,
What will be inside?
It better be finished soon
Before the big year arrives.

So let's thank God
For all He's done,
It will soon be 2000 years,
From when He sent His Son.

Grace Frazer (11)
Edendale Primary School

THE DOME

The Dome is going up,
Excitement all around,
The Dome is going up and up,
In good old London town.

People shall come from all around,
To see this wonderful sight,
There shall be lots and lots of new things,
All shining in millennium light.

We hope and pray that God will bless us,
Over the next one thousand years.

Rachel Stewart (11)
Edendale Primary School

FASHION IN THE MILLENNIUM

I wonder what fashion might be like,
It's a mystery to me.
So if you want to find out
Just you wait and see.

People might wear short skirts,
Or they could wear old old shoes.
They could wear hipsters or leggings,
But you never know what they might
Choose.

You'll never know what it will be like,
Until the 12 strikes of 1999 have gone,
We'll never know what will change,
Until that day will dawn.

Kathryn Cromie (11)
Edendale Primary School

THE YEAR 2000

The millennium will be fun,
With lots of different things,
Like a new Millennium Dome,
And with all the things it brings.

I hope the millennium will be good,
We are going to have a party,
Lots to eat and lots of fun,
And everyone feeling hearty.

David Cromie (10)
Edendale Primary School

OUR PETS

Our home has become a chaotic place.
Everywhere - a hairy face!
In from school - flat on the ground,
Staring up at a hairy hound!

Timmy the Tripod is so mad
There is not one bit of peace to be had.
He licks your face and bites your toes,
You may protest but on he goes.

Patch is quiet, not so bad,
In fact she looks a little sad.
She's rather old, but fit as a flea
But when she plays it's quietly.

Sophie is a ginger cat,
One year old and getting fat
Still she likes to join the fun
Playing about with everyone.

Richard Kavanagh (11)
Grange Park Primary School

SUMMER

Bees buzzing around the flowers,
Working busily for many hours.

Birds singing with the morning dawns,
Daisies growing on everyone's lawns.

Building sandcastles on the sand,
And getting ice-cream from an
Ice-cream van.

Julie Hanson (11)
Grange Park Primary School

ANIMAL TALK

Bears growl, wolves howl,
doves coo, cows moo.
Animal sounds, down to the ground,
Cockerels crow, oxen low.

There are cats, frogs,
Horses and dogs
Making a different sound each day,
Did I mention donkeys bray?
Go with the hum of the bees!

With a cackle, a quack and a cluck,
In comes the geese, the hen and a quack of the duck.
There goes the elephant please join me now,
In with the *Animal Sounds*.

Bears growl, wolves howl,
Doves coo, cows moo.
Animal sounds, down to the ground
Cockerels crow, oxen low.

Kayleigh Richardson (11)
Grange Park Primary School

THE BARGAIN HUNTERS

There they go!
They search in the window,
They prowl in the shops,
Their bodies tense,
Their eyes are keen,
They search, they stalk,
They find their prey.
The *biggest* bargain in town!

Lorna Montgomery (11)
Grange Park Primary School

MANCHESTER UNITED

I support Manchester United FC
They're better than Chelsea.
They're the best team on Earth,
A fortune they are worth.

They're going to win the double,
If you play them you're in trouble.
Yorke and Cole are the best,
They score goals past the rest.

They play in red and white,
To watch them is a delight.
Alex Ferguson is the boss.
Without them football would be chaos.

James Farnham (11)
Grange Park Primary School

SHUT YOUR GOB!

There was once a boy that always talked,
When he did he would like to mock,
The kids that weren't very good,
At spelling, sums or making stuff with wood.

He said to the illiterate,
'Ha Ha, you can't read,'
He said to the new kid,
'Ha Ha you don't know the school creed.'

Now the new kid whose name was Lou,
Thought about what he was going to do.
He was very shy so all he said was,
'Bob, shut your gob!'

Tom O'Hara (11)
Grange Park Primary School

LIFE

(From a teenager's point of view)

Being a teenager is such a drag
You wake up with your eyes like bags.
The work at school is so boring
You're woken up by a friend to be told you were snoring.
When you get spots
You usually get lots and lots.
You have to revise for hours and hours
For that stupid exam of yours.
No McDonald's because you're broke,
But school dinners, they make you choke.
You're trying to do your revision
But your sister asks for help with her division.
It's not fair that swimming and hockey are on the same day
You have to carry your stuff all the way.
But nobody cares.

Naomi Pollock (11)
Grange Park Primary School

WHAT IS A FRIEND?

A friend is one who's
Always there.
A friend is one who
Always cares.

A friend is one who
Trusts me.
A friend is nearly
Part of the family.

A friend is one who
Helps me through.
A friend is one
Whom I like very much.

A friend is called Naomi
Who does all these things.
A friend to me is honest
And holds on through
Good and bad.

Joanne Chestnutt (11)
Kilmaine Primary School

MY PONY DAVEY

I have a little pony
His name is Davey boy.

He really is so lovely
He is my pride and joy.

Each day we go a cantering
Around the field and tracks.

And when the weather is much better
We go on very long hacks.

Oh to enter competitions
Around the country I go.

I have won trophies, cups
and lots of rosettes.

I think that ponies
Are the very best of pets.

Jenni Brittain (11)
Kilmaine Primary School

SCHOOL SWAPPING

Of all the things that happen,
Changing schools is the worst
Some teachers will be missed of course,
But others will be cursed.

New friends and new beginnings,
But old friends' contacts, keep on thinning.

Now is the time for new languages to be learnt,
Science, English, maths,
Old textbooks to be burnt.

Now I must put my brain into gear,
But where on earth will I steer?

Kerry Watton (10)
Kilmaine Primary School

CHRISTMAS

Christmas is a time for loving,
Christmas is a time for giving,
Christmas is a time for sharing,
To remember that Christ was born,
Time to decorate the trees with lights,
Burning showers are oh so bright.

Cosy beside the fire, watching television,
Pitter-patter on the windowpane,
Lying in bed not a peep,
Presents and gifts to open today,
I'm going to play in every way
31st December, another year has come and gone.

Erin Leslie Todd (11)
Kilmaine Primary School

A DAFFODIL IN THE GARDEN

A daffodil in the garden,
So dainty and light.

A daffodil in the garden,
Trumpet-shaped yellow and white.

A daffodil in the garden
A flower that blooms in spring.

A daffodil in the garden,
So pretty, I sing.

A daffodil in the garden
Summer comes and it dies,
But next year he will come out
To play again.

Rachael Brady (11)
Kilmaine Primary School

NIGHT

It is black.
I am scared,
The shadows are moving,
I am sweating.
I need to get up,
The night drifts slowly.
I feel fear.
I am still scared.
I am trembling in fright.
Then I hear my mum call me.
Then everything is right.

Andrew Bingham (10)
Kirkistown Primary School

THE DESTRUCTIVE WIND

I am staring out the window watching
The destructive wind
Bashing the trees
From side to side,
Throwing the birds about in the air.

There is howling,
Whirring and whistling.
I hear the sea
Pushing over the walls.
The seaweed is pushing up too
And I am watching
The destructive wind.

James Douglas (10)
Kirkistown Primary School

THE BLACK SHEET

I lie in bed too scared to move
The night is being cruel.
It's black and scary
It's so silent and still
I hear footsteps
I freeze with fright
But my fear drifts away
Because sunlight is taking over.
It lifts the black sheet and throws
                    it away.
I hear my mum call me
I give a sigh of relief.

Jolene Palmer (10)
Kirkistown Primary School

IF I MOVED HOUSE

If I moved house
I would take
The day I got my puppies
But I wouldn't take
The day I was in the garden
And I slid
And fell face first
Into the mud!
I would take
The time Regan widdled into Dad's shoe!
He was very mad!
I wouldn't take the time
Jolene, Melissa and I
Went exploring through the fields
We got very dirty!
I would take the time
Mummy woke me and told me Rachael was
Born.
I remember the time
When my dogs had a fight
In the yard
I wouldn't take that!
But I would take the time
When my dog first got bathed.
He soaked everywhere
Even me!

Emma Anderson (10)
Kirkistown Primary School

WIND

The wind is a fox!
Sly and cunning.
Slipping in unseen!
Slipping in unheard,
Stealing something.
Then slipping out,
Unseen, unheard.

The wind is a bully,
Nasty and up to no good.
Barging in raging.
Barging in shouting,
Causing destruction,
Then barging out,
Raging, shouting.

I don't care what the wind is,
Fox or bully,
It can't scare me!

Tanith-Yola Finegan (11)
Kirkistown Primary School

I WILL NOT LET YOU IN

I will not let you in wind!
You can blow the slates off.
But I will not let you in.
You blow dust into my eyes.
You blow leaves up at my face.
And that is why I will not let you in!

Ryan Maginnes (10)
Kirkistown Primary School

WIND

The wind is a lion!
It prowls through the trees.
I am tucked up in bed
I say, 'You cannot get me!'
The wind roars.
Rain smashes
On the roof.
Wind pounds
On the road.
Trees fall
On the path.
Wind is a bully!
There is silence.
There is a *bang*.
The sea crashes
Over the wall.

Victoria Adair (9)
Kirkistown Primary School

THE WIND

The wind bullies the trees,
They get tossed about.
The wind gets angrier and angrier.
It blows the seas over the steep walls.
The wind swirls the lost leaves
And plays with them.
It blows rubbish down the street.
The wind is satisfied with its work!
He is thinking a new plan
To destroy the Earth.

Gareth Graham (11)
Kirkistown Primary School

HAUNTED BY NIGHT

As I lie in bed wide awake
I can hear the deafening silence.
The world has closed a curtain on the day
A black mysterious world.
I can see the moon's light,
Streaming through the window.
As I lie there
The day starts to slowly come through
Like a flower opening up.
As the morning lights up my room
I am struck with relief.
I'm not scared!

Alison Brown (10)
Kirkistown Primary School

DARKNESS

It was night.
It had crept up on me.
I was scared.
It seemed spooky.
It was silent.
I heard noises.
I saw branches of trees.
I saw strange shadows.
Then the darkness faded away.
Slowly morning came.
The town woke up.

Rebecca Peden (9)
Kirkistown Primary School

A STORM

The wind is very angry,
It is determined to demolish trees
The wind is grey.
It rattles and howls ferociously
Demolishing trees and fences
That blocks roads.
The storm is like a battlefield.
It howls, rattles and bangs.
And it is raining.
I lie in bed listening
While my dad is going to work
Cutting up branches.

Steven Evans (8)
Kirkistown Primary School

A STORM

The wind punched the window
I was scared!
The rain flooded everywhere.
I was lying in bed.
The covers were up round me.
I was scared!
The trees danced with the wind.
It pushed them over like a baby
It's like a fist of wind.
A knuckle of rain
The stars go mad when dawn comes.

Zoe Adair (10)
Kirkistown Primary School

WILD WIND

The wind is angry
The sun is away behind the black clouds.
Thunder and lightning strikes.
Wind blows down trees.
It is like a monster blowing all the trees.
It blows down houses.
Leaves blow all around us.
The wind is a bully to all of us.
The sea is bursting over the wall.
The wind is spoiled!
It does what it wants.

Brian Cromie (9)
Kirkistown Primary School

IT IS DARK

The night tiptoes by.
It invades us.
It is still.
Everything is black.
You see the trees swaying
back and forth.
I can see the shadow of my
cat in the window,
and I am scared.

George Edward Calvert (10)
Kirkistown Primary School

Let's Celebrate!

The millennium is coming,
Everyone will celebrate,
It's gonna be exciting
It's really gonna be great.

There'll be balloons and streamers
And coloured paper flowers,
It's gonna be a great night,
We'll celebrate for hours.

Music blaring in the street,
Food being passed around,
Just say the word mill-enn-ium,
'Cause it's a lovely sound.

Emma Johnston (11)
Milltown Primary School

Surfing The Net

Don't you love to surf the Net
On a computer screen
Click the mouse and press a key
And see things never seen

Sit down and turn it on
For a world of fascination
Lots and lots of gossip
And maybe information.

All your favourite pop stars
Have got a Web Site
So get linked on to find out more
And have a really good night.

Graham Woods (11)
Milltown Primary School

MY TEDDY

I have a teddy and he is three.
All day long he talks to me.
He has brown eyes and dark brown fur.
He has a round head
and a bare patch that has always been there.

Every morning he comes down for tea
He sits on his chair and stares at me.
He gulps it down fast
And then goes out.
He goes fishing for a while,
And then comes home with a big trout.

Then at night he goes to bed.
He has a small pillow to rest his head.
He snores all night long,
In the tune of a song.
He made it up himself,
On March the twelfth.

Michelle Crangle (11)
Milltown Primary School

2000

Everybody talked about it,
Robbie Williams wrote a song about it,
They probably wrote books about it!
Now it's here,
The 2 thousandth year,
And we all begin to celebrate.

We open the gate,
To all our friends,
Who come to have some fun,
We open the bottles of Shloer,
When we finish our sight's a blur.
Because it's the year 2000!

Eunice Dunlop (11)
Milltown Primary School

WHAT IS THE RAIN?

The rain is Heaven's water pipes,
Throwing out its waste.

The rain is God's precious gems,
And people collecting them with haste.

The rain is glittering snowflakes
Telling children to come out and play.

The rain is sparkling silver fish,
Landing in the pond where a yellowish ball
Once lay.

The rain is the twinkling stars,
Falling from a dark blue web.

Hannah McGookin (11)
Portaferry Integrated Primary School

BEYOND 2000

Land covered with cities
Lifts to far away galaxies
Life on other planets
Cinema widescreens for everyone
PlayStation 5000
Robots turn evil
Wars between robots and humans
Time machines for history in school
The sky black with all the pollution
Trips to the centre of the Earth.

If I'm right?
Talk to me in 50 years

Andrew McDowell (10)
Portaferry Integrated Primary School

WHAT IS RAIN?

Rain is blue paint splattered
On a white page
Rain is diamonds falling
From the sky
Rain is someone smashing
Glass in Heaven
Rain is small meteorites
Falling from space
Rain is peas falling from
God's plate.

Peter Savage (10)
Portaferry Integrated Primary School

BEYOND 2000

People's purses filled with cash.
Cars drive by themselves.
People begin to fly.
Old people walk fast.
Earth, the smartest planet.
Children at school on the Internet.
Everything made of chocolate.
Shopping malls on the moon.
Every animal free.
Cars at 600 mph.

Would this happen?

Let's see!

Jervais Ashmore (11)
Portaferry Integrated Primary School

BEYOND 2000

A never-ending story
A football that never bursts
A bike that never gets punctured
A shuttle to space, no need for special suits,
Cities on other planets.
They might wake up and realise
That genetically modified food can kill.
Will this happen or will they not?
I suppose I will just have to wait and see.

James Reid (8)
Portaferry Integrated Primary School

IT'S COMING - MILLENNIUM

Millennium is
A new future for us
A time when pigs fly in the air
A big party all over the world
A place with no pollution

Big cinema TVs in our homes
New computer inventions
A new life for everyone
A complete nightmare
Bugs in machines
Whatever it is,
I'm glad to be part of it.

Zoe Gilmore (9)
Portaferry Integrated Primary School

IT'S NEARLY THE MILLENNIUM

It's only 2 days away
Until the big day
Count down the time from Big Ben
So get out a bottle of wine and then
Have a party. It's time to improve this world now.
With a hover car or a hover cycle
Computers that talk to you.
I think I'm going to enjoy this millennium.

Hugh Mathews
Portaferry Integrated Primary School

Millennium Is

Millennium is
No smoking
A time of joy
Peace on Earth
Computers that talk to you
A never-ending time
Pop-up buildings
People on Mars
Get ready for a surprise
We don't know what's in store.

Jonathan Reid
Portaferry Integrated Primary School

Beyond 2000

Cinema televisions in our homes
Computer consoles too
Solar-powered or even battery cars.

Beyond 2000
More or less pollutions?
People may walk on Mars,
A smoke-free world - maybe!
Beyond 2000

I hope I live to see what happens.

Andrew McCluskey
Portaferry Integrated Primary School

BEYOND 2000

Beyond 2000 will there still be Global warming?
Will there be cinemas in our homes?
Will cars use solar power?
Will children learn to drive?
Will people stop smoking cigarettes?
Will there be less pollution?

Will this happen?
I will just have
To wait and see!

Charlene Ott (11)
Portaferry Integrated Primary School

BEYOND 2000

Beyond 2000
Will I be rich?
Will it be bad or good?
Aliens will come, they'll eat the people, yum yum yum.
Will we die?
Will we love or will we lie?
Where will we be?
Can we have bigger TVs?
Well that's the future, something I can't see,
I guess I'll just have to wait.

Mary-Jo Ellison (10)
Portaferry Integrated Primary School

PLEASE HAVE PEACE

I am sitting here, thinking
While out there they are fighting.
Shooting, bombing, killing
What is the point of war?
They are just fighting to get their way.
If they win they won't be the
Champions of the world.
People die, their families are losing
Members of the family.
For once stop and look around,
You are destroying the world.
I am sitting here, thinking
While out there they are trying to
                                    have peace.

Please stop!

Rebecca Best (10)
Poyntzpass Primary School

MILLENNIUM

Once again the millennium has come
1000 years have passed
We celebrate and have parties too
We shout and sing alleluia alleluia
We jump and we yell
We run and we fall
That's the fun we have
My dad had a bit of Scottish beer that night
My mum stayed at home and baked the bread
My sister was out with her boyfriend
But my brother was out with me.

Colin Reaney (11)
Poyntzpass Primary School

CONSERVATION 2000

Look after the birds.
Especially the rare ones.
Don't trap them,
Don't shoot them,
Just don't kill them at all
Feed them on seeds.
Keep them as pets if you like.
Feed them and breed them,
Then release them,
And let their numbers grow,
Don't let your pets kill them
We've got homes
So don't destroy their homes
Or don't leave your fishing
Tackle or rubbish behind.
Or you could put up bird boxes
And leave them out scraps.
For all little birds are important to us.

James Hammond (10)
Poyntzpass Primary School

PEACE

Here I am sitting worrying myself sick
About my family and myself
People screaming, hearts jumping
I can't take my mind off peace

Children screaming for their mums
I wonder if that would be me
Discovering that their family are dead
I can't take my mind off peace

Animals running everywhere
Looking for their mums as well
What an awful world this is.

I hope the fighting will stop and
The world will be a peaceful place
For you and *me.*

Neil Liggett (10)
Poyntzpass Primary School

FIVE, FOUR, THREE, TWO, ONE

Dark covers the sky
As midnight begins to come
Bangers go up in the sky.
As hands begin to drum
Now is the time
Five, four, three, two, one
Happy millennium.

Ban drugs and bugs
Tobacco too.
Ban weapons
Ban hunting rare animals.
Plant more trees
And catch more thieves!
The millennium is full of joy and hope
Everyone is amazed today has come.

Debbie Long (10)
Poyntzpass Primary School

IF MY BROTHER . . .

If my brother was an animal,
He'd be a big, bad dog.
Scraping around and making
The most annoying sounds.

If my brother was a place,
He'd be an erupting volcano.
With a bright, red face,
And a very bad temper.

If my brother was a colour.
He'd be a very dark red.
Like a red-hot poker,
Or a fire blazing in the woods.

If my brother was a food,
He'd be a red-hot chilli.
Steaming with anger.
Then getting very hot.

Steven Boal (11)
Redburn Primary School

WINTER MORNING

The morning comes, we look outside,
Frozen puddles, a quilt of snow,
Freezing snowballs, numb hands.
People with hankies sneezing,
The sound of chilling coughing,
The knives of coldness strike me,
When I long to go inside.

Luke Somerville (10)
Redburn Primary School

IN BED AT NIGHT

My hamster fixing its bed,
Footsteps on the landing,
Weird creaking noises from the attic,
My heart starts pounding, I freeze.
The clothes on my door turn into a person,
Glaring at me.
I look at the ceiling, I see a snake and
Turn on the bedside lamp.
Phew! It's only a shadow.
I lie down, I hear the radiator clanking,
I stop breathing, and listen.
I hear myself breathe very fast,
I look in the mirror, it flashes.
I see the creepy moonlight,
Staring back at me.

Adam Makhfoudi (9)
Redburn Primary School

ICE

I see puddles that have hardened into smooth ice,
The roads have grit on them to stop cars skidding
Into other cars,
The trees are bare and have turned from brown to white,
A pond has frozen but has thin, sharp cracks,
The grass has frozen and when you stand on it,
It cracks under your feet,
I feel excited and want to slide,
The clothes on the line are stiff and hard,
My ears go red and my fingers are numb,
I desperately long to go inside.

David Moore (11)
Redburn Primary School

SOUNDS AND SIGHTS AT NIGHT

I hear the wind howling
The rain crashing
I hear footsteps squelching in the rain.

The floorboards start creaking
My breathing gets louder and louder.
My heart starts beating harder and harder
I squeeze myself together and hope there's
                                    nobody there.

I see a large, creepy, unidentified shadow
But luckily enough it's my brother
Fidgeting, waiting for the toilet.

The water tank sounds as if it wants to be fed
It's dribbling and gurgling
The tap is letting out its leftovers
Clicking and trickling.

When I turn the light on
I discover there's nothing there
It's all in my imagination.

Rachael Walker (11)
Redburn Primary School

MY MUM

If my mum was a material
She'd be a piece of silk
Soft, gentle and
Smooth against my skin.

If my mum was an animal
She'd be a cat
Friendly, never angry
Sitting on the sofa.

If my mum was a place
She'd be Connswater
Always busy
Rushing off her feet.

If my mum was a bird
She'd be a robin
Small and pretty
Cheeping around the garden.

Charlene Mallett (11)
Redburn Primary School

MY UNCLE

If my uncle was a place
He'd be a volcano
Erupting all the time
And his temper would be red and hot.

If my uncle was weather
He'd be a fierce storm
With thunder and lightning
And dark blue, heavy rain.

If my uncle was a food
He'd be curry
Spicy and very hot
Ready to burn you when you touch him.

If my uncle was an animal
He'd be a German Shepherd
Who wants to eat you for his dinner
And every other meal.

John Stephenson (11)
Redburn Primary School

In The Night

The wind is howling and whistling
The rain is dribbling on my windowpane
Strange footsteps in the sticky mud,
My rabbit is digging a hole in the grass.

Floorboards are creaking
Water tank groans
A shadowy figure on my closet door
My heart stops beating,
I hide under my covers
Phew! It's only some coat hangers.

Radiators keep clicking and clanking
Lights are starting to flicker
Taps are dripping into the kitchen basin
The fridge is humming all night long.

Terri Reid (10)
Redburn Primary School

My Colour Poem

Black is evil.
It makes me feel spooky
It tastes like witches brew
It smells like smoke in the night
And echoes in the dark.
It looks like shadows in the dark
And makes me feel terrified.

Jonathan Entwistle (9)
Redburn Primary School

LONELINESS

Loneliness is blue,
Loneliness is walking round and round
Wondering if someone will come,

Locked up in my room alone
All there is, is the sweet sound of birds,

Everyone playing in the sun having fun,
And me standing near the window
Watching them play,

I'm waiting and waiting for someone to come.

Stuart Botham (11)
Redburn Primary School

MY COLOUR POEM

Pink is friendly.
It makes me feel relaxed and sleepy
Pink tastes like an ice-cream and a black crispy flake on top.
Then I am dancing on air.
At a beautiful fair.
It smells like perfume.
Pink is a flower in my garden.
It sounds like music falling from the sky.
Pink is kind and pretty.

Mary-Jayne Goodwin (9)
Redburn Primary School

MY COLOUR POEM

Green is thoughtful
It looks like a stick insect hanging from a tree
Green is like an open forest
Green makes me feel like I'm in the park
Green makes me very happy
Green looks like a snapping tortoise
Green is very pleasant and very joyful
Like mint and lime so quiet and smooth.

Victoria Vine (8)
Redburn Primary School

MILLENNIUM

No matter where I wander, no matter where I go,
All the talk is about the millennium,
I'm not looking forward to it! No!
We might have to change our computers,
The machines in our home might not work,
The planes in the sky might fall on our rug,
Because of the Millennium Bug.
This bug will be hard to find,
It cannot be killed with spray
I know it's on everyone's mind
But all you can do is pray!

Clare O'Callaghan
St Brigid's Primary School, Newry

THE YEAR 2000

Celebration 2000 we have so much fun
We have no fears
With fun and games it's coming near.

Money goes in, money goes out
New things are coming
So we all run about

New things are coming
New things are near
What fun it will be this 2000 year

The lights will go out but I don't care
Because all my toys will be there
The Bug will cause all this stuff
Or is the Bug just a bluff?

Stephen Campbell (9)
St Brigid's Primary School, Newry

NATURE!

Nature is hot, nature is
Green, nature is full of
Life.
Birds are singing and
Dancing all around.
The cows are mooing
And eating the fresh
Green, green grass.

Aidan Garvey (11)
St Brigid's Primary School, Newry

MILLENNIUM 2000

Although it is only a date on a calendar.
It is a day most people are looking forward to.
With newspaper coverage and media hike.
We all know what will be going on.
Counting the days, and the days rolling by.
We all hope it will be, what we like.
Although the day will be short the night will be long.
Accompanied with excitement, music and song.
When it's all over we ourselves will not see its like again.
It will be like the last flicker of a light at the end of a day.
This day will not come for another thousand years.
So take great heart and dry up your tears and sing
                    with Robbie, the song Millennium.

Daniel Garvey (10)
St Brigid's Primary School, Newry

CELEBRATING 2000

The Millennium Bug is like a drug,
When it gets into your blood.
People wonder, people shrug,
The year 2000 will it be smug?

Where will we be in the new century?
Some say without electricity.
But for me, it will be,
Brilliant to see.
Ring in the new century.

Amy Bradley (10)
St Brigid's Primary School, Newry

MILLENNIUM

The 19th century is in the past.
Year 2000 has come at last
We will all celebrate
Because this is a special date.

I hope in the future
We can have peace.
We want no more fighting
And the trouble to cease.

The millennium is a special time
We shall all have fun
We've been preparing for a year
Now it has just begun.

Ladean Rowland (9)
St Brigid's Primary School, Newry

MAYBE

Maybe things could show us through,
Maybe it would help us do.
Maybe it could help us feel.
A thing that we could share a meal.

Maybe peace will rule the land,
All the fighting stopped and banned,
Maybe things would be a dream,
Maybe the sun would shine like a beam.

Donna Reel
St Brigid's Primary School, Newry

MILLENNIUM MADNESS

Millennium madness is soon to come,
The 1900s are nearly done.
Millennium is the name,
Celebrating is the game.
Great changes all around.
New inventions will be found,
But there are some people sure to worry.
As the Millennium Bug will come round in a hurry.

Evanna Kieran (9)
St Brigid's Primary School, Newry

CELEBRATION 2000

New Year's Eve, 3, 2, 1,
'99 out, 2000 Just begun.
There will be a party,
Sweets and pop,
Cheers and laughter
From everyone.

Lisa Walsh
St Brigid's Primary School, Newry

YEAR 2000

Millennium is on its way
So we say for that day
That we will change in our ways
And hope and pray for peace
To last throughout all year 2000

Carla McShane
St Brigid's Primary School, Newry

MILLENNIUM

I hope there is peace for the millennium,
For me and for you.
For this is a time,
For peace and joy too.

New people are born,
New things are here,
And we can sense
Millennium is near,
> near
> near
> *Here!*

Katie Harvey
St Brigid's Primary School, Newry

MILLENNIUM

M is for music, everyone dancing,
I   is for illness, the Millennium Bug,
L is for leisure, being sporty,
L is labs, new technology.
E is electricity, computers and TVs go out
N is for numbers, school numbers increasing.
N is for no, the Peace Agreement goes on,
I   is for inventions, new things are made.
U is for Ulster, reuniting families,
M is for madness, everyone party.

Caoimhe Murphy
St Brigid's Primary School, Newry

MILLENNIUM

Oh! The millennium will be so much fun toys and
Games for everyone dancing and marching
On the street, oh what a wonderful treat.

Singing songs having fun food and drink
For everyone's children playing and running about
Then we hear a mighty shout, it's time for
Our countdown.
5 4 3 2 1, oh the new millennium has just
Begun. Good wishes to everyone.

Thomas Walsh (9)
St Brigid's Primary School, Newry

HALLOWE'EN

I'm looking out my window on
This starry Hallowe'en night and the
Things that I am seeing are a
Truly wonderful sight.
Splashes of blue and red and green
Lighting up the sky on Hallowe'en
First the bang and then the
Eruption of colour cascading down
Like falling stars.
The smoke-filled sky soon clears
And all that remains are the
Twinkling of stars and the gleam
Of the moon.

Claire Heatley (10)
St Clare's Primary School, Newry

SISTERS

Sisters, sisters, they all are pains,
Like the weather when it rains.
Stealing toys,
Just like boys.
Chasing us round the house
Just like a squeaky mouse.

Sisters, sisters, they all are funny
Like the weather when it is sunny
Sharing sweets
Giving me treats.
Playing with me inside and out
Making sure I'm always about.

Deirbhile Murphy (10)
St Clare's Primary School, Newry

SCAMPER

My Grandparents' dog is small and tan,
He goes with them in their Camper Van.
A holiday away or shopping for the day
A well-travelled dog one might say
He goes for a drive along the coasts
But loves the sandy beaches most
He plays with a rubber bone on the floor
And is always alert when there's a knock on the door
He lies along the top of a chair
With attentive ears up in the air
If you see him you will find
Cute and cuddly, one of a kind.

Shauna McParland (10)
St Clare's Primary School, Newry

THE PLAYGROUND

The playground is an exciting place
For me, you and others.
With slides and swings and dirty faces
And no other bothers.

My friends and I play lots of games
That last for hours and hours
We sometimes fight and call each other names
But when we are hungry we buy crisps and bars.

At the end of the day
When we all go home
We can all say
We've had a nice day
And we'll never be alone.

Natasha Kearns (11)
St Clare's Primary School, Newry

MY MUM

My mum is nice.
She always makes rice.
I love my mum she is
Sweeter than a plum.
She always buys me things,
Such as gold rings.
I love my mum I will
Never forget her goodness,
Kindness, and caring for me.
I love my mum very much.

Margaret Lisa Ward (11)
St Clare's Primary School, Newry

MY SISTER

My big sister is very tall
And when I'm beside her I feel
Quite small,
When I'm sick she cares for me
She makes my bed and makes me tea
Although sometimes we shout
And fight
But when I'm with her I
Feel alright.

Clare Rafferty (10)
St Clare's Primary School, Newry

TO WRITE A POEM

I tried I tried
I thought I sighed
I moaned I groaned
My brain my hand disowned
My sweat was running
Five minutes to go, I looked at this page
And I shouted wow!

Claire McMurray (10)
St Clare's Primary School, Newry

THE MOON

M is for the moon coming out
O is for oh! The moon does not have any light of its own
O is for once every four weeks the moon goes round the Earth
N is for new light the moon makes.

Nicole Doran (8)
St Colman's Primary School, Moira

EASTER

Easter is a happy time
Eating Easter eggs all day

Eggs in red paper, eggs in gold, not getting
Eggs until you are told.

I picked an egg and Mum said 'Are you sure
That's the one you want,
Because I'm not staying here for an Easter egg hunt.'

Asking Mummy when the Easter bunny was coming
To the street.

You'd better go and find him as fast as you can
On your feet.

Danielle Mallon (9)
St Colman's Primary School, Moira

TUG OF WAR

Tug of war is the game for me,
Pulling and puffing,
Getting quite warm,
Pulling very hard,
I get the most rope,
She pulls most of it off me,
I get a bit off her,
Then she pulls too hard,
The rope leaves me,
She has won this game,
Why don't we play again?

Caroline McArdle (8)
St Colman's Primary School, Moira

EASTER

E ggs to eat at Easter.
A sking Mum for my Easter egg now.
S tarting to put Easter eggs in shop windows.
T rying not to be sick with too much chocolate.
E ating tasty Easter eggs.
R unning to the toilet being sick.

Jennifer Hull (8)
St Colman's Primary School, Moira

CARS

I wish I had a fast car
they can drive pretty far.
The new Clio with fancy seats
it also gives out cool beats.
355 is really cool
if you don't drive one you're a fool.
Dodge Viper it's in my dreams
in the sunlight it will gleam.
Subaru Impreza 555
it's raring to go and really live.
Nissan Skylight is so sleek
of course it wouldn't leak.
McLaren F1 noisy and fast
if you spin in it you wouldn't last.
Aston Martin DB7
if I drove in it, I would be in heaven.
V12 engines - speed galore
they have even got suede floors.

Keith Forsythe (10)
St John's Primary School, Hillsborough

TEACHERS

Teachers steal all your pens
and most of them need contact lens.
Pupils getting sore heads because teachers break
your good pencil leads.
They put a lot of make-up on
to attract the men that come into the school.
Not most teachers have a BMW.
I think it was part of my teacher's pay rise.
I think my teachers are very casual and
they don't treat you sometimes like a pupil.
Sometimes teachers act like fools
but I think my teachers are quite cool.
Mr Morrow is so cool
if you don't like him - you're a fool.

Victoria Brown (10)
St John's Primary School, Hillsborough

MY BABY BROTHER

I love my little brother
he's not a bit of bother.
But I wouldn't want another
neither would my mother!
He's worth a million dollars
his skin is soft and sweet.
And he's started eating meat
and even his little feet!
He has a new walk-about seat
it's like a car and it's got a clutch.
He loves it very much.
His name is Harry Brown
and I couldn't do without him.

Natalie Brown (10)
St John's Primary School, Hillsborough

THE MARAKITE

His eyes go click
His mouth goes crunch.
He looks at you and sees *lunch!*
The children cry and the women squeal
But all of them became his meal.

He sends the birds flying
And leaves the babies crying.
And in the night you should hear the snore
It's an almighty *roar!*
In the morning you'll hear him yawn
He'll wake you up at the strike of dawn.

So if you hear a deafening *roar*
Or the wind rattling on your door
Just hide in your bed
Never go outside or you'll be dead!

Jonathan Walker (11)
St John's Primary School, Hillsborough

OLD TRAFFORD

Go on Scholes - score more goals
Stam's got a nestt - which is the best?
According to Fergie, they've conquered
Europe
David's got a child, which is the best.
Schmeichel's got a hand which saves like mad.
Cole and Yorke are scoring like lads.
Henning's got the touch for his feet
                saving the ball off the line.

Nevin Spence (8)
St John's Primary School, Hillsborough

MRS MOP

Mrs Mop would sweep the house,
She might see the odd mouse.
She sweeps round and round
She sweeps all the crumbs off the ground.

She dusts all around the door,
She moves and does some more.
She sweeps up and down,
She's so good, she deserves a queen's crown.

She is a women turned upside down,
When you turn her round you might hear a screaming sound.
She cleans everywhere she goes,
How she cleans so well - no one knows!

Christopher Walker (9)
St John's Primary School, Hillsborough

SPIDERS

It's getting warmer every day
lambs skipping in the sun.
Poppies, daffodils, buttercups and daisies
no more rain or damp - but we get spiders.
But the worst are bees and wasps and spiders.
March, April, May is spring.
I can't wait for it to come
but the worst are spiders.
I hope it's sunny this year
It's supposed to be good this year
because on St Patrick's Day - it's a good day.

Emily Kennedy (9)
St John's Primary School, Hillsborough

ANIMAL TALKING

Animal talking is very weird
it may be a neigh or a miaow.
People might be able to speak
People might not.
They might be able to speak monkey language
with a little ooh-ooh and another ooh-ooh.
They might jump in the air
They might not jump in the air
They might neigh to speak to a horse
with a little neigh, neigh.
They might have clever little machines
They might not have machines.
People might be clever making new machines
People might just talk.
Pretending to be able to speak to the animals
People might just talk to them
just because they love them.
We don't know what they'll do
we don't know anything.
We just watch to see what people know.
People might just talk and talk
Tell people what to do.
We can do what we want
like horses getting ridden a lot.
So they do what they want
tell what they want
until they finish work.

Abigail Allen (8)
St John's Primary School, Hillsborough

A TREE

Once I saw a little tree
that stood still most of the day.
It blew with the wind and rain and cold.
I liked to watch that little tree every day.

I watch the boys and girls
climb that little tree.
Climb that little tree
it's the best in the whole big town.
Not just the children climb the tree
I do just as much as the children do
I am just 9 not 18
I am not that old
I am 9 years younger than 18
Not 18 yet
I suppose I am a child yet.

Amy Oliver (8)
St John's Primary School, Hillsborough

IF I WERE . . .

If I were a squirrel
I'd live in a big tree
And see all around
Bound to be something special for me
Sleeping sound
Then I'd wake up to a bright light
Not a person in sight
Kites are flying high in the sky
Children are buying lots of sweets
Seats are needed for mums and dads
Sitting down they have their tea
Then it's bedtime for the children
Clothes line is down
Everybody is sound asleep.

If I were a cat
I'd live in a big house
And chase lots of mice
Sit by the fire all day long
And be stroked and loved
All day long
I have to go to sleep.

Ruth Megarry (11)
St John's Primary School, Hillsborough

EASTER

Oh, the Easter bunny
his ears are really quite funny.
Jesus was crucified
and Judas lied.
We roll eggs down a hill
just like what happened to Jack and Jill.
Easter dates back to the Celts
sometimes our chocolate melts.
Caiaphas saw
how Jesus questioned their law.
Leading people astray
yes Jesus got in his way.
Simon was an African man
but he didn't plan
to carry his cross.
Easter is a time to celebrate
Oh, I can't wait.
Jesus wore a crown of thorns
the Easter Egg represents the newborn.

Andrew Simpson (10)
St John's Primary School, Hillsborough

MY PUPPY

My puppy is nice, he's brown and white.
He goes outside and plays with me,
Ben my dog bites me on the leg,
My dog is soft and lovely and cute,
I feed the dog and lead the dog,
My dog is called Ben,
I like that name,
I don't cry but I sometimes lie about my dog,
I am going to bring him into school,
I hope he won't be a fool.

Judith Caldwell (8)
St John's Primary School, Hillsborough

EASTER

I like Easter - it is cool
Eggs are everywhere
Eggs are cool to roll down a hill
Easter is lovely, chocolate eggs are lovely
Jesus was crucified at Easter
Sometimes our chocolate melts
But chocolate eggs are too good to waste
I like white chocolate.

Samuel Ward (10)
St John's Primary School, Hillsborough

THE YEAR 2000

I am a river
        long and wide
with stepping stones
        to climb
from side to side.

I have seen the ancient
        people walk
along the side
        of the rock.

I have seen people
        fall in love
with romance.
        kiss and hug.

I have watched
        the time go past
and watched the
        time change so
now I'm ready
        to look forward
to the new
        millennium.

Karanne McCartan (11)
St Joseph's Primary School, Crossgar

CELEBRATION 2000

I have watched upon the Earth
for years and years and years on end.
And each day it seems the world has started
all over again.
I've seen all the Royals
take their place
upon the throne with
manner and grace.
I have watched the
wars and atrocities
start and finish.
The children of the future
should live a happy life.
Never again should they see
a bullet, gun or knife.
So let's have a party
Let's hear 3 cheers
For we're about to begin
Another 1000 years.

Caoimhe McErlane (11)
St Joseph's Primary School, Crossgar

CELEBRATION 2000

I am the sun of sea and sky
I watch you all the time
and I have seen all that's in the past.
I am around the Earth
I have seen the moon shine
I want to see the Earth for
another 1000 years.

Nicole Lynch (10)
St Joseph's Primary School, Crossgar

CELEBRATION 2000

I am the Sun
I've shone on this Earth for
millions of years.
I have shone on this Earth
and look forward to shining
come the dawn of the new
millennium.

Goodbye to the old and welcome
to the new century.
I have given the world light
and I shall continue that.
I am looking forward to witnessing
the changes, inventions and advances.

Mark Bell (11)
St Joseph's Primary School, Crossgar

2000 YEARS

For 2000 years I've looked at the Earth.
I've seen it evolve from its birth.
Over the years I've seen the animals
change shape and size because of mankind.
But 2000 years may bring
extraordinary things like . . .
People flying
Others gliding
Cities and towns flying in space
Looking for another human race.
But 2000 years may bring tears.
What will the next 2000 years bring?

Thomas Ward (10)
St Joseph's Primary School, Crossgar

THE MILLENNIUM

Everyone is talking about the millennium.
I wonder what all the fuss is about?
I suppose after 1000 years we have
something to celebrate!
There's no place like the Dome for the millennium.
The big bowl in London stands proud.
When completed in the year 2000
it hopes to attract a big crowd.
It can hold two Wembley Stadiums,
or the Eiffel Tower on its side.
What a magnificent building.
It's 300 metres wide!

Anna McKeown (11)
St Joseph's Primary School, Crossgar

CELEBRATION 2000

I am a river
        long and wide
                meandering along . . .
Twisting, turning, splashing, babbling.
As I flow on my way I see many changes.
The people come and go
The trees grow taller
The new birds sing a new song.

Long ago people waded barefoot in me.
Now fast cars and trains go above me
on big heavy bridges.

Long ago people would wash in me
and swim in me.
Now they have baths and pools to use.
I have experienced many things over
the past 2000 years.
Now it's time to celebrate the new
                Millennium!

Lauren Casement (11)
St Joseph's Primary School, Crossgar

CELEBRATION 2000

My stone walls have stood one thousand years
and another thousand years they shall stand.

My lands have changed hands many times,
through battles and wars.
Kings and Lords have fought for my lands.

In the past I had candles but now I have electricity.
I have witnessed inventions,
Gutenberg's press, Edison's bulb.
My halls are haunted with generations of the past,
Victorians, Normans and Georgians.

The next thousand years hold mystery and surprise,
I could meet my end or see the Starship Enterprise.

Here's to the next thousand years and let
there be one thousand more!

Kevin Bell (11)
St Joseph's Primary School, Crossgar

POEM FOR THE YEAR 2000

Over the years
I have seen
things that only
you would dream.

As a spirit
you may know
I, God
was born long ago.

Since my Son
had his quiet birth
there have been changes
on this Earth

Wars, battles,
travel in space
are some of the things
that made the human race.

People have done
well over the years
but what is to come
is the top of my fears.

Conor McCartan (10)
St Joseph's Primary School, Crossgar

THE CELEBRATION 2000

God sent me
down to keep
people alive.
I'm a part of everyone
I make their heart pump
blood around
their body.
I have been
part of the
Royal family.
I have been
part of the rich
and poor.
I have seen people
breathe me no more.
I have seen people
breathe me
once more.
I hope to see
another
millennium.
I am the breath of life!

Claire McCartan (10)
St Joseph's Primary School, Crossgar

TESY

Tesy is a wonderful cook,
she really doesn't need a book.
She gives us dinners every day,
in a very special way.
She always has a smile on her face,
and keeps up a really good pace.
We will be sad to see her go
because we will miss her so.
We all wish she could stay
as she is special in a way.
Watching her cook the food,
makes me think she is so good.
No one thinks her food is bad.
She has to go - that makes me sad.

Carole Trueman (11)
St Joseph's Primary School, Downpatrick

SNOW

Snow, snow, snow is good
even if you're in a bad mood.
Snow is thick and nice and white.
When the sun comes out
it is very bright.
When the snow falls
on the ground.
We dance and sing
all around.
But now our poem
has to end.
We'll be back
next weekend.

Lynn Colhoun (9)
St Joseph's Primary School, Downpatrick

HALLOWE'EN

On Hallowe'en night
you're in for a fright.
You'll never know
what will come up.
I creep in my bed
with my pillow over
my head.
And wait for the
morning to come up.
When the clock
strikes twelve.
In the blankets I delve.
I lie in my bed
and wish I was dead.

Leanne Murray (10)
St Joseph's Primary School, Downpatrick

THE SNOWMAN

I love to make a snowman
really, really big.
Sometimes I put on him a big red wig.
He has a carrot for his nose
it was a red one, which I chose.
But he doesn't wear belts
I hate when the sun comes out
because he melts.
When I get up in the morning
it's a sunny day.
But when I go outside,
the snowman had melted away.

Colette Lowry (9)
St Joseph's Primary School, Downpatrick

SNOWFLAKE

Snowflake, snowflake
you are so light.
Snowflake, snowflake
you wouldn't bite.
Snowflake, snowflake
you are so white.
Snowflake, snowflake
you are like a kite.
Spinning and floating
drifting down.
Falling, twirling about
he's acting like a clown.
Dancing about in the sky
it seems like it can fly.

Nolene Trainor (10)
St Joseph's Primary School, Downpatrick

STORM

Thunder, thunder I hear you.
Thunder, thunder do you
hear me too.
Lightning, lightning you are
bright,
Lightning, lightning on a
scary night.
Thunder and lightning
what a mix
Thunder and lightning do
your tricks.

Orlaith Killen (10)
St Joseph's Primary School, Downpatrick

MY GRANNY
(The Day That Granny Was Cross)

Here's my granny . . .
Look at you, you look a fright.
Look at your jeans
they're covered in muck.
That pony tail
what do you look like?
A fright.
Oh! I'm not.

Dinner, yum yum
gobble gobble.
Your clothes are a mess.
Run back home and get some clean clothes
Oh! Alright!

I'm going out to play
I come back in.
Granny I've lost my hair bobble
Go to your room.
Hello mummy, let's go home!

Hannah Lucas (8)
St Joseph's Primary School, Downpatrick

ICY DAY

I saw some ice outside and got it
And brought it to the classroom
And put it on my table and it melted
And melted and melted.

Emma Lavery (9)
St Joseph's Primary School, Killough

THE CUP

On Saturday there
was a football match.
I got on for the first
half.
We were one goal down
until I scored a goal.
When it was half-time
I was off the pitch.
Then we had a penalty
competition.
It was the end of the match.
We were wondering who
won the Cup:
And I know now . . . us!
We all celebrated with the Cup.

Aodhan Fitzsimmons (8)
St Joseph's Primary School, Killough

THE SCARY DREAM

The water drips from the ceiling
and there are cracks in the wall.
No one in the house, no one at all.
There's gunge coming through the cracks,
I'm shivering under my bed -
feeling that there are ghosts around my head.
I'm stiff as a rock and it's dark outside -
footsteps on the street - I hide.
But a hand comes through the window.
I try to scream -
But I realise it's
A dream.

Adam Holmes (8)
St Joseph's Primary School, Killough

TIGER

Once I was born it was all over.
I didn't know what the world was.
The next thing I knew a hunter shot my mother.
I was so astonished.
Then some zookeepers saw me,
they took me to their zoo.
It was heaven,
there they fed me,
the finest quality meat and fish.
Then one night, robbers came
and they stole me!
I was dead
Well at least nearly!
Then they shot me.
I was so unhappy when they shot my mum,
but now they have shot me -
all for my fur coat.
Do I need it more than you do?

Sinead Burns (8)
St Joseph's Primary School, Killough

THE CREEPY BARN

In the old barn
The ceiling drips and the floors go
Flip
Flap
Swish
They lead you into a cellar where
The ghosts
Hide.

David Hackett (8)
St Joseph's Primary School, Killough

MY PUPPY

I've got a new dog called Whiskey
and when my friends all heard of her
they thought she was a drink.
But there's some bad news now . . .

She has to go!
Oh no!

I feel so terrible about this happening.
She has to go because she bites.
But at least she's going to a good home.
I will miss her very much.
Oh, I feel like I'm going to cry!

My daddy knows the woman
who is taking her.
So I can go and visit her
anytime I want.
But I am still disappointed.

I will never forget about you Whiskey
and I hope you never forget about me!

Natalie McGowan (9)
St Joseph's Primary School, Killough

MY BEST FRIEND

My best friend is Sally
she's a very good friend to me.
She often comes to our house
just to have her tea.

We eat lots of chips and burgers
and always have a laugh.
By the time we're finished playing
we both do need a bath.

We have been friends since playschool
and had never had a row.
Until the day I told her
she was a silly cow.

She screamed and yelled and hit me.
It made me very sad.
But that day now is over
and we are very glad.

Shirley Briggs (10)
St Joseph's Primary School, Killough

FAVOURITES

Sometimes I'm sad,
sometimes I'm happy.
When I'm sad I sit all alone and
when I'm happy I spring from a rose.

When my mum sits all alone
I go and cuddle her and keep her warm
and snuggle up tight
and don't let the bedbugs bite.

My doll sits all alone
all by himself.
No friends at all to play with
or to talk to.

My dad sits all alone
I love him so very much.
I don't know what to do.
I don't know when to sit on his knee
in case he bites me.
Or leave him alone.

Nicola Laird (10)
St Joseph's Primary School, Killough

A TRIP TO THE WOODS

One night I asked my parents 'Can I go tonight?'
My parents said 'Yes.'
I got my tent and then I called my friends.

You guessed it!
We were going camping.

When all four of us got to
the woods it was nearly dark.

We set up the tents and made a campfire.
We all sat down to eat.
Oh, so brave and courageous.

I heard a rustling over there!
No, over there!
Out jumped a tiger!

We all ran home, never looked back.
But now we know never to go back to the woods
in case we meet another tiger - or was it a wild cat?
Or a fox or . . .
Mrs Smith's kitten!

Kieran Burns (9)
St Joseph's Primary School, Killough

THE DIAMOND GROUND

The diamond ground so white and clear,
The footsteps cracking that I could hear.
The frost that sparkles on the ground,
The wind that blows all around.
There was a fresh feeling inside,
And my hands in my pockets that I had to hide.
The sight of the ice, the wind that blew,
It was so cold. What could I do?
Then the sun came out and all was done,
Although the frost had just begun.
The ice is gone,
And it is dawn . . .
And the sun shone down upon the ground,
But sure it's winter all around!

Laura Braniff (9)
St Joseph's Primary School, Killough

SCHOOL

In our school there's a boy called Jim
he has a friend called Tim.
In school they go into the gym
and one day Jim stood on a pin.
When he got to hospital
the cost was quite a lot.
When he got back to school
he got lines
and it said
You must not go into the gym!

Stephen Black (9)
St Joseph's Primary School, Killough

HIDING AWAY

Hiding away on the
deck of a boat
it is so horrid and
grim. The floorboards
creak and there's fish guts
on the side, a little
homesick, a little
of hunger. I wish
I had some food.
The crew are grumpy
up in the Nest watching
for schools of fish
Helping themselves to
a snack. The blue whale
blows out water while
the boats fill with people.
The whale swims on and
the boats come back with
blood and anger. But right
now I have to settle down
to sleep among some
rags.

Rachel Sharvin (10)
St Joseph's Primary School, Killough

THE MONSTER

Jack the monster
Lived in a forest
He could never see light
By day or night.

He would walk a million miles,
Just for one of the sun's smiles.
He's very sad,
But he's a big brave lad.

But if somebody
Would just help him
For a while
Let him have a smile.

In winter he can't even
See the white
Of the snow
Somebody help him 'Go, go, go!'

And in the summer
He sits alone
In his forest cage
Nobody cares.

Cunliffe Fitzsimmons (9)
St Joseph's Primary School, Killough

JACK FROST HAS COME

I was surprised to hear
My teacher say 'Today is the day we go out to play.'
And I just wasn't surprised,
Everybody was.
We ran to the window
And saw the frost and ice.
I got a shiver from head to toe
And we let out a squeal,
Turned and shouted 'Hip, hip hurrah!
We are going out today.'
So we got in line
Marched into the yard
While falling, slipping, twisting and turning
There was black ice here
And black ice there.

There was ice, frost and black ice everywhere.
It was just beautiful when the sun was shining on the grass.
But because it was so icy, everyone was so cold,
And when we went into class, we were soaking.

Grainne Cupples (8)
St Joseph's Primary School, Killough

THE FROSTY MORNING

Today we went outside
And found some amazing things.
I found some frosty leaves
They were absolutely icy,
Then I found lots of ice
In a puddle. Padraig stuck his foot in.
All the ice cracked;
I found a frozen worm.
I walked on the grass
Creaking; creaking;
Then we all came in
From outside because it was getting
Very cold and we came in to write about
Outside.

Oonagh Kelly (8)
St Joseph's Primary School, Killough

CRUNCHY GRASS

One morning I woke
Up and went to school.
'Hard work! Oh no!'
We went outside
To see what the ice looked like.
We went on the grass
And it crunched.
Then we went in and I felt
Freezing!

Brady Magee (8)
St Joseph's Primary School, Killough

THE WORLD OF ICE

When I went outside
I could hardly breathe.
I had to take a couple of breaths
Before I could breathe.
My ears were frozen so I could not hear.
I stood mouth opened,
My nose was red,
My toes were numb.
When I came inside,
I thought I was invisible,
I said, 'Radiator! Radiator!'
And I felt myself reappear.

Aoifa McEvoy (9)
St Joseph's Primary School, Killough

SCHOOL

I was only four
When I first walked through the door
I felt so small
When I went into the dining hall

I learned my A, B, Cs
And my 1, 2, 3s
I liked to play
And have my say

I am now eleven
I am just finishing primary seven
It will soon be time to go
So I will have to say 'Cheerio.'

Nicola O'Callaghan (11)
St Laurence O'Toole's Primary School, Newry

THE LION

Morning dawns,
The lion yawns,
He spots his daily kill,
A little gazelle.

His bones sticking out of his chest,
He isn't at all his very best,
So anxious to eat,
He's tired of the heat.

To gain his weight,
He really needs to eat,
Vultures surround him,
The sky getting dim.

A heavy rain storm,
The gazelle lets out another yawn,
The lion's luck is up,
He begins to look.

He searches for food,
He's not in a good mood,
So you better hurry,
Or you'll be 'sorry'!

The lion gives up,
He falls to the muck,
Flies cover him all over,
Now his life is over.

The vultures fly in,
In for the kill,
The blood running out,
The day is almost out.

John Savage (11)
St Laurence O'Toole's Primary School, Newry

MYSELF

My hair is black,
My eyes are blue,
My name is Louise,
I don't like bees.

I am not too fat,
I am not too thin,
I like Irish dancing,
And I like to swim.

I have two sisters,
Sometimes they are a 'pest',
We laugh, play and fight,
But I still think they are the best.

Louise Helen Smith (9)
St Laurence O'Toole's Primary School, Newry

MY DAY

Up at eight, I can't be late,
Mummy leaves me at the school gate.

Another day has begun,
I hope I have all my homework done.

With my friends I will have fun,
We can play jump and run.

At my desk I sit and listen,
I hear and see all that is spoken and written,
For to all my subjects I am smitten.

Caoimhe Quinn (8)
St Laurence O'Toole's Primary School, Newry

SPRING

Spring is nice
Not like ice.
In spring I go away to a cottage.
To keep me full I get some porridge.
Flowers grow with no snow.
The sun shines
With yellow lines.
Buds grow on trees
With honeybees.
Sometimes they go buzz
Maybe even fuzz.

Jenny Rafferty (7)
St Laurence O'Toole's Primary School, Newry

MY FRIEND

My friend has black hair,
He makes me laugh,
He runs and shouts,
Like a little calf.

If my friend is thin,
If my friend is fat,
I like my friend,
And that is that.

Dane Hayes (10)
St Laurence O'Toole's Primary School, Newry

LUCKY BREAK

In the morning when I get out of bed,
I dress for school which I usually dread.
It's to the bathroom in a dash,
Where I brush my hair and have a wash.

Then to the table for tea and toast,
When Mum remarks 'You look like a ghost.'
I explain I don't feel too well,
Hoping she'll say, 'Stay at home, what the hell!'

But no such luck as I pack my bag,
Mum's finger begins to wag.
'Hurry now, or you'll be late,
Your lift is waiting at the gate.'

As I'm walking out towards the door,
Something falls onto the floor.
Oh what an idiot I have been,
It's a note from school I haven't seen.

Please beware there is no school today,
As you may not know it's a holiday.
I cannot believe what I have read,
As I turn around and head back to bed.

Rachel Rafferty (10)
St Laurence O'Toole's Primary School, Newry

STAR

I wish I was a little star shining in the sky
I wish I was a little star and twinkle in your eye
I wish I was a little star shining very bright
I hope you see this little star twinkle in the night.

Nishia Hayes (8)
St Laurence O'Toole's Primary School, Newry

MY DOG

My dog always fights with ducks,
But that is when he has bad luck,
He often plays in the garden,
That's my dog, my little darling,
He sometimes is cross,
He soon shows who is boss,
I love my dog,
Whose name is Tod,
He is spot on,
And I would not like to see him gone.

Shane O'Hare (10)
St Laurence O'Toole's Primary School, Newry

MY DOG

I have a little dog
His name is Toby
I feed him every evening after school
And I take him for a walk
He meets me every evening, coming home from school
He is very friendly
He would come with me anywhere
I made a little kennel
He runs in when it is raining.

John Hearty (8)
St Laurence O'Toole's Primary School, Newry

MY SPECS

My eyes are dim, I cannot see,
For I have not got my specs with me.
I need my specs to read and write,
Otherwise I cannot do it right.
I use my specs to watch TV,
If I hadn't got them I could not see.

Kelly-Marie Smith (9)
St Laurence O'Toole's Primary School, Newry

HALLOWE'EN NIGHT

Hallowe'en night will give you a fright,
the biggest fright of your life!

Children beware, you're in for a scare.
ghosts and ghouls are transparent fools
they'll pull down your knickers
they really are sickers.

Here comes the vampire, bloody and old
he's bit people for centuries so beware!
Look out for the zombies, here comes one now
they're flesh-eating monsters, so run!

The nasty old witch with her scary black cat
that pimpled old nose she won't smell like a rose,
demons, devils, spirits and goblins.
Watch out for these abnormal creatures!
On Hallowe'en night.

Darragh McCambridge (11)
St Mary's Primary School, Banbridge

THE FALLING LEAF

I'm hanging on the edge of a branch,
Ready to fall and dance.
Then I'm fluttering down,
Until I reach the ground.

Then all at once I have fluttered down,
I have met my friend with a crown.
They all had a party going on,
It was in the lawn.

Then Mrs Wind came along,
She danced and sang a song.
So we danced and sang,
The party is all yours and mine.

Now, I'm crinkled up in a ball,
It was just three weeks ago I was ready to fall.
Now I'm a dead one too,
So, come back autumn so I can play with you.

Kerri Winters (9)
St Mary's Primary School, Banbridge

SPRING

When spring comes it's hard work for bugs
The birds lay their eggs
Squirrels jump from tree to tree
Lambs are playing happily
Spiders eating daddy-long-legs
Winds and storms and sunny days
Squirrels knock down their winter dreys.

Paul Downey (8)
St Mary's Primary School, Banbridge

MY HEAD

In it there is a thought,
A thought of cats and dogs,
Endless days of playtime, sleeping like a log,

The grass is green,
The sky is blue,
There's a lot of things for me to do.

Birds sing and rabbits jump,
Fun for one and all,
Hide-and-seek and rollerblades, jumping off a wall.

Swimming at the seaside,
Fishing on the lake,
Drink a lot of lemonade, eat a lot of cake.

These are thoughts inside my head,
Of very special days,
Thoughts I will remember, for always.

Kris McGrath (10)
St Mary's Primary School, Banbridge

SPRING

When spring comes, bright is the sun,
The spiders' webs are almost spun.
The birds are all making nests,
Mrs Butterfly is having guests.
Squirrels climbing up the trees,
Buzzing wasps and honey bees.
Flowers blooming all around,
As in the fields lambs are found.

Lucy Hillen (8)
St Mary's Primary School, Banbridge

TO HAVE A LITTLE BUNGALOW

Oh to have a little bungalow!
To own a PlayStation, TV and all!
A heaped up pile of compact discs,
The ghettoblaster against the wall.

To have a poster of Roy Keane,
The white and red, the mighty Pete,
A United quilt, Celtic pyjamas,
A radiator and lots of heat.

And when I come in home from school,
A bag of crisps, a cup of tea,
Bart and Homer on the telly,
That's what half three means to me.

But when I'm tired, cold and wet,
If I'm sick or feeling low,
There's nowhere else I want to be,
But home in my wee bungalow.

Lochlainn Hill (9)
St Mary's Primary School, Banbridge

MUSIC

M usic is a wonderful thing
U sing the tin whistle
S ome music is soft
I   love the claves
C laves are my favourite instrument.

Tara Purdy (7)
St Mary's Primary School, Banbridge

THE POOR ALLEY MAN

Away in the corner,
In the dark of the street,
Sits the poor alley man,
With no shoes on his feet.

All sad and alone,
With no one to talk to,
And no food to eat,
He can barely walk.

Oh what wonders he could do,
With a bit of cash,
He could buy some potatoes,
And eat them as mash.
But he has no money,
To spend on food,
Because of people,
Who are greedy and crude.

So it's back to his corner,
To sit and hope,
That he earns some money,
To help him cope.

Daniel Smith (11)
St Mary's Primary School, Banbridge

WINTER

If winter would be spring,
The daffodils would ring.
I would jump in snow,
To hurt my little toe.

Conor Maginn (6)
St Mary's Primary School, Banbridge

THE BUNGALOW OF MY DREAMS

Oh to have a little bungalow!
To own the cooker, fridge and all!
To own a lovely, cosy bed,
With a lovely patterned wall.

To have a little fence!
To paint it dark brown!
To go and do my shopping,
In the little town.

To sit in a comfortable sofa
And watch my favourite soaps,
And if I had a husband,
He'd own a little boat.

To own a little puppy,
I will love him with care,
To own a little hairdryer,
For my lovely golden hair.

Sarah Murphy (10)
St Mary's Primary School, Banbridge

WINTER

If winter was
called every season
and it snowed everyday,
Winter would be my
best season ever.

Taylor Kearney (6)
St Mary's Primary School, Banbridge

SCHOOL

It starts at
9.00 and it
finishes at 3.00

All day long
the teachers are
shouting.

We do English
maths and all
the other boring things.

Then the
bell
goes.

Bye, bye
teachers,
Ha! Ha! Ha!

Caroline McCusker (10)
St Mary's Primary School, Banbridge

WINTER

Once I met a snowman.
He sure was white with snow.
I taught him how to talk
and I taught him how to walk.
He came into my house one day
and he melted by the radiator
and then we had a funeral for him.

John Kearns (7)
St Mary's Primary School, Banbridge

SPRING

S pring is full of joy, sun shining.
P rancing birds, lambs bleating, baby chicks.
R abbits playing in the meadows and
I n danger, foxes chasing the lambs.
N aughty foxes. The little lambs died. Horses
G alloping through the fields.

Mark Pearce (8)
St Mary's Primary School, Banbridge

WINTER

W inter is the coldest season.
I cy and snowy and lovely too.
N ice and cold for kids to play in.
T hick enough to write your name in.
E ven the adults building snowmen
R unning and jumping and playing about.

Connor Quinn (8)
St Mary's Primary School, Banbridge

WINTER

The hands of God
cover the world
with white snow.
When the children
come out they have a fright
and start a snowball fight.

Ciara Dunleavy (7)
St Mary's Primary School, Banbridge

SPAIN

S pain is a very hot country!
P eople are very nice too.
A t night the disco is on.
I think the beach is nice too.
N ow I have to go, I hope you liked Spain too.

Gareth Smith (8)
St Mary's Primary School, Banbridge

SCHOOL

S ome people are bad
C urious and nosy
H eadmaster cross with them
O pening doors for visitors
O n the ground lost money
L ooking for lost money, oh dear we cannot find it.

Áine Donnelly (8)
St Mary's Primary School, Banbridge

SPRING

In the springtime every flower blooms.
In the springtime new birth begins for new little animals.
In the springtime you leap so do the other animals.
You feel so fresh in the spring.
Oh, oh I dream of spring.

Francesca McQuaid (7)
St Mary's Primary School, Banbridge

AUTUMN GONE AGAIN

I wish I was part of an evergreen tree,
Then this cold wind couldn't blow me.
Red, yellow, orange and gold,
The colours of autumn are taking hold.

Misty, frosty, windy and wet,
That's the weather that we get.

Spinning softly in the air,
Twirling, whirling everywhere.
The leaves floating to the earth below,
Know that it is time to go.

It's sad to leave this old oak tree,
It will have no cover without me.
It doesn't know what the weather will bring,
But leaves will return in the spring.

Sarah McClean (10)
St Mary's Primary School, Banbridge

ARCHERY

A rrows going everywhere.
R apid shots from good archers.
C hallenging for the prize.
H ilarious bad shots.
E agle-eyed and observant.
R unning when not allowed.
Y ards from the target they try and try.

Oisín Martin (8)
St Mary's Primary School, Banbridge

THE VAGRANT

Oh to have a little bungalow!
To own the cooker, fridge and all!
The milk is left upon the door,
And your dog for you to call!

Your car is parked outside!
Waiting for you to drive!
The children are playing outside,
It would feel like you were just alive!

I've got a garden filled with flowers!
They're standing there as good as gold,
The people walking by would stare
At my little house which is very bold!

I would have a lovely bed!
To lie in all night,
I would have lots of lovely books
I think I would be alright!

If I had my little bungalow,
It would be great!
I would be happy all day long,
I suppose it's just fate!

Oh to have a little bungalow!

Bronagh Campbell (10)
St Mary's Primary School, Banbridge

BLOOD ON HIS HANDS

It's Hallowe'en night at 10.36pm,
I thought I saw the Devil,
He had blood on his hands.

It's now 11pm, I'm doing my shift at the quarry,
I'm sure I saw Demo-Goblin,
He had blood on his hands.

It's now 11.55pm, I'm in the graveyard, visiting uncle Tom.
Ahh! It's zombies, demons, banshees, ghouls, vampires,
Skeletons and werewolves and they all have blood on their hands!

Phew! It's 3am. It was a dream,
But what's that thing beside my bed,
It's got blood on its hands . . . *ahh!*

Stephen Downey (11)
St Mary's Primary School, Banbridge

INSIDE MY HEAD

I have two eyes, two ears, a mouth, a nose.
I use my forehead to score a goal.
My lips are small, my teeth complete.
My tongue goes *ah!* in sheer defeat.
This young boy's head so full of dreams.
Hopes to succeed before his teens.
To enjoy each day as a young boy should.
Being happy, being healthy and being good.

Shane Nelson (9)
St Mary's Primary School, Banbridge

WITCH'S SPELL

Tonight is my cauldron night
With all my things I'll give a fright
Mouldy porridge, lumpy custard
And a bit of bread and mustard
A bat's wing and an old man's hat
A shark's fin and an itchy mat
A dog's ear and a cat's eye
A skeleton's leg and a nice juicy fly
A frog's tongue and a newt's toe
A sweaty sock and a lizard slow
A squirt of gunge and an old woman's nail
Oh! What a spell for Bronagh Quail!

Catherine Cunningham (10)
St Mary's Primary School, Banbridge

AUTUMN'S JOYS

Autumn's joys are wonderful things,
In autumn comes the misty rings,
There are apples, pears and blackberries,
In autumn grows the poisonous cherries,
In autumn grows wheat, barley and acorns,
So watch out for those prickly thorns,
There are leaves as nice as red and brown,
Which grow in almost any town,
I just want to say goodbye,
So watch out closely with your eye.

Gary Buchanan (10)
St Mary's Primary School, Banbridge

A Frosty Morning

One cold, icy morning,
I got up from my bed,
I heard a little voice
From inside my head.

It said 'The roads are very slippery,
There is nowhere for you to go,
Because there might be a chance
For it to snow.'

The children are out
Playing about,
You better watch out,
He'll be out tonight!

Corinne Jordan (11)
St Mary's Primary School, Banbridge

A Frosty Morning

It's a frosty morning,
And there's ice about,
It's slippery and slidy,
So watch out, watch out,
The ice is sparkling very bright!

Jack Frost has been out,
The road is slippery and slidey,
The path is like a crystal in
                    the bath.

Dana Kane (11)
St Mary's Primary School, Banbridge

TWENTY-TWO FOR HILL!

Five lights
Four lights
Three lights
Two lights
One light
Only three seconds
Go! Go! Go!
Pole position for Damon Hill
Into first place he goes
Eddie's in second
Schumacher in third
Murray's excited
As the cars speed past.

Lap number eight
Sees Schumacher in first
Passing Damon at the bus stop
Murray is silent
Coulthard puts Shumy out
Anything can happen
Rain! Rain! Rain!
Tyres need changing
Damon keeps his lead
Speeds around the chicanes
One lap left to go
Yes! Yes! Yes!
Damon's won
His first Grand Prix of '98
The Belgian Grand Prix
Bringing his total to twenty two.

James Doran (10)
St Mary's Primary School, Banbridge

MY BEDROOM

My bedroom
I'm proud to say
is a tip, and I actually
prefer it that way.

People have their rooms
neat and prim
but when mine's like that
it makes me feel *grim*.

It's my room so why
should anyone care
even if it was a mess
or in it there was a lion or a bear?

Ruth Mulvenna (11)
St Mary's Primary School, Banbridge

JACK FROST

Jack Frost is out
He's out to give you a bite
He's cold, he's icy,
So beware and
Don't dare to go out.

Jack Frost is out
He's chilly and nippy
He's black and he's white
He will give you a bite.

Jack Frost is out
So stay in your beds
Tonight.

Carla McArdle (10)
St Mary's Primary School, Banbridge

SHARK

Masters of the sea,
Their dark black eyes,
Jaws open wide,
Chomp!

Fish,
Swim at your peril,
Sharks are about,
And it's dinner time.

Tiger, hammer head,
Great white, blue,
All the same,
Bloodthirsty,
Masters of the sea.

Andrew Lavery (11)
St Mary's Primary School, Banbridge

WINTER

Oh winter is here at last
at last, so long have
I waited so now
I will go out and play
now that it is here.
The snow is cold
and the air is nippy
on my toes.

It is fun out here
in the snow
but a day later it
was gone. But so
much fun I had in
the snow.

Anna McArdle (10)
St Mary's Primary School, Banbridge

WINTER

This is December,
the day I'll remember,
snow is falling everywhere,
it's falling down onto my hair.

Jack Frost is out,
he's jumping about,
he's here, he's there,
he's everywhere.

Rain comes to the ground,
with a big thunderous sound,
the children splashing, having fun,
making lots of work for Mum.

Stephen Hynes (10)
St Mary's Primary School, Banbridge

THE SUN

Flares like a bonfire on Hallowe'en night
Glows like cats' eyes staring at you up a
        tree
Sparkles like an angel's wand flying across
        the sky
Drips like a melting lollipop sitting on the
        ground
Shines like a stream flowing down a
        mountain
Smiles like a beautiful sunflower growing in
        a meadow
Floats like a golden hot-air balloon across a
        sea-blue sky.

Emma Boyle (9)
St Mary's Primary School, Killyleagh

THE LIVING CARS

The buildings are like people
watching the animals.

The lion cub's roar is like
a motorbike zooming by.
The buses and lorries are
the cub's dad and mum.

All the horns are all
the roaring animals.

These animals are all nocturnal.

Paul Woodside (11)
St Mary's Primary School, Killyleagh

SPRING

Something told the bear
it was time to wake up.
He opened his eyes and
it was bright once again.

Something told the sheep and pigs
it was time to have their babies.

Something told the buds
it was time to pop
and bring out little green leaves
to make a beautiful tree.

But something told the weather
to change to sun
so children can play
and have some fun!

Jacqlin Brown (9)
St Mary's Primary School, Killyleagh

RUSTLE BUSTLE

A lorry pushes its way by
Like an elephant. The traffic
Lights are spying in case
Someone tries not to stop.
A bus reminds me of a monster
That eats people and rushes
To the next stop to get more.
Engines rev that is the rustle and bustle.

David Gregge (11)
St Mary's Primary School, Killyleagh

ALL ALONE

Walking alone in the dark
The moon is like a dim torch light
Silhouettes of trees coming after me
The trees - big twisting ropes
Darkness crawling all around me
Wolves howling,
Owls hooting
I'd better run, run fast
At last I get through the door,
And shut the darkness out
Safe in my bed, I will gladly sleep.

Kirsty Nelson (11)
St Mary's Primary School, Killyleagh

MY BROTHER

He is as fast as a car
He looks like a dog
He loves to drink coke
John likes football and golf
John thinks he is a singer because
He sings *The Full Monty*
Every time he comes home from
School he is like a bull
If John was in the zoo he should
Be with the lions.

Adele Gribben (11)
St Mary's Primary School, Killyleagh

THE STARS

Twinkle in the bright black air.
Shine in the black sky beside each other.
Glow after sunset and go at sunrise.
At Christmas the bright yellow star
sparkles to lead the way to Bethlehem.
The ordinary stars come out each
night shimmering in the air.

Steven Fegan (8)
St Mary's Primary School, Killyleagh

THE SUN

Shines like a ring on your finger.
Sparkles like a golden key in a castle.
Twinkles like a dancing fire burning in the grate.
Glows like a magic pea in a fairy tale.
Lights like flame burning in the night.
Gleams like a pot of gold.

Louise McGreevy (8)
St Mary's Primary School, Killyleagh

THE MOON

The moon glows like a lamp in the dark.
Shines like a dragon's glowing eyes.
Lights up like a pot of treasure.
Glimmers like a sparkling silver ball.
Glistens over the rooftops like a bowl of golden water.

Kirsty Coughlin (8)
St Mary's Primary School, Killyleagh

STARS

Glow like diamonds on a blue dress.
Sparkle like glittery make-up.
Twinkle like a frozen lake.
Brighten the sky like fireworks shooting up.
Gleam like new jewels.
Sparkle like gold buttons on a king's jacket.
Flash like car headlights.

Kathryn Clark (9)
St Mary's Primary School, Killyleagh

THE STARS

Glow like a candle in the darkness.
Sparkle like a crystal ball.
Shine like a polished mirror.
Twinkle like a magic key.
Gleam like gold coins.
Brighten like a fire at midnight.

Gary Morrison (8)
St Mary's Primary School, Killyleagh

THE SUN

Blazes like a yellow marble rolling across a blue floor.
Burns like a yellow football kicked across the sky.
Fries like a chip pan burning chips.
Jangles like a golden earring.
Flows like scorching sand on the beach.

Connor Quinn (9)
St Mary's Primary School, Killyleagh

SPRING'S SONG

Something told the buds,
it's time to open your shoots.
Time to let your beautiful leaves
spread around.

Grow your reddest roses
around the greenest grass
shining in the sun like
a heart for your Valentine.

Something told the birds
it was time to fly back
to meet their mates
and sing along with them again.

They fly back from distant lands
and build their nests
to keep their eggs safe
from the crowds and hawks.

Danielle Doyle (9)
St Mary's Primary School, Killyleagh

STARS

Glitter like sparkly nail polish.
Wink like lots of icicles hanging from the roof of a cave.
Shimmer like a sheet of shiny silver paper blowing in the wind.
Sparkle like freshly brushed teeth.
Glisten like a fountain of pretty pearls.
Gleam like a snowflake falling from the sky.
Twinkle like a crown of water drops.
Glow like a stream of ice.
Dazzle like a line of angels dancing.

Lori Cheevers (9)
St Mary's Primary School, Killyleagh

SPRINGTIME

Something told the bear
it was time to yawn
time to find nuts and berries
and stretch on somebody's lawn.

Time to meet up with old friends
and amble down the street.
Catch up on the old times
although sleeping are your feet.

Something told the humming bird
it was time to come.
Time to lay an egg or two,
We missed your lovely hum.

Build a nest and
sing your heart out.
If you want a mate
it won't be long, I have no doubt.

Something told the snow
to melt away down.
Wait until another winter
so we won't have a frown.

Slouching on the garden path
turning into mush.
When the sun comes out
it will be nothing but slush.

John Higgins (9)
St Mary's Primary School, Killyleagh

SPRING'S SONG

Something told the pale green buds
it was time to sprout.
It was spring
without a doubt.

Something told the wild birds
it was time to return.
Time to fly back home,
to their forest fern.

Baby animals are born anew,
something only mother animals can do.
They have to feed and wash them,
if they're hungry they won't shoo.
Something told the flowers,
it was time to grow.
Don't put too much water in the pot
so they won't overflow.

But something told the weather
it was time to change.
Instead of being very freezy,
how about a little breezy?

Nadine Corrin (9)
St Mary's Primary School, Killyleagh

SPRING

Something told the daffodils
it was time to grow
so they pushed their way
up through the soil and spread
their petals in the breeze.

Something told the birds
to get a friend and build a nest.

Something told the buds
to grow into big leaves
and turn green.

Something told the
animals to wake up and
find their food.

Something told the
weather to go warm.
But something told the ewe
to have a baby lamb.

Ashleen Carson (8)
St Mary's Primary School, Killyleagh

THE STARS

Glow like fireworks in the night.
Shine like lights in houses.
Sparkle like diamonds.
Flash like lights on a fire engine.
Twinkle like crystal balls.

Shane Adair (7)
St Mary's Primary School, Killyleagh

SPRING

Something told the sheep
it was time to have baby lambs
to skip, run and hop
around the field.

Something told the birds
it was time to lay eggs
and teach the baby birds
how to fly in the sky.

Something told the buds
it was time to grow.
Time to bloom lovely bluebells.

Danielle Nelson (7)
St Mary's Primary School, Killyleagh

SPRING

Something told the animals
to wake up.
It was time to get food.

Something told the ewe
to let her baby lamb be born.

Something told the new buds
they had to burst and change colour.
But something told the birds to sing
and wake us all up in the morning.

Vicky Bennett (8)
St Mary's Primary School, Killyleagh

SPRING

Something told the buds
it was time to grow.
The new buds pushed their way up
and grew new leaves.

Something told the birds
it was time to return.
To find a mate to lay
eggs then they can
be a happy family.

Something told the flowers
it was time to grow.
They are so beautiful
the daffodils, tulips, snowdrops,
primroses and bluebells.

The weather is getting warmer
the birds are singing in the trees.
The mother sheep are looking after
their baby lambs.
They drink some milk from their
mothers then hop and skip away.

Dean McComb (8)
St Mary's Primary School, Killyleagh

STARS

Sparkle like fireworks in the gloomy air.
Twinkle like a silver dress with some shiny sequins.
Glow like a chalice in a darkened church.
Glisten like a new gold ring.
Flash like a shimmering candle in the window.

Sorcha Walsh (8)
St Mary's Primary School, Killyleagh

SPRING

Something told the animals
it was time to wake up,
time to have something special
like a beautiful baby pup.

Run to the river that flows,
get ice-cold water to drink.
Running and dancing along
go into your house that's pink.

Something told the birds
it was time to come back,
return from migrating
and tell us a bit of your crack.

Fly along in the bright blue sky,
find yourself a mate,
sing your song and lay some eggs
before it is too late.

Now the buds are back,
the trees are not so bare.
They rustle in the gentle breeze
but you should know I still care.

Caroline Walker (8)
St Mary's Primary School, Killyleagh

THE STARS

Glow like a glittery dress at a party.
Twinkle like diamond rings in a shop window.
Sparkle like a polished floor in the evening.
Shine like a candle burning in the darkness.

Joanne Sullivan (7)
St Mary's Primary School, Killyleagh

THE SEA

The sea is a rushing animal,
leaping everywhere.
Rough waves come bounding in and hit off the sandy rocks.
White foam floats upon the surface,
as the sunlight shoots into the sea.
Children jump and paddle along the thundering waves.
Screeching gulls dive into the water
as salty ripples jump with a splash.
Smells of rotting seaweed crackle beneath.
Eventually the water is calm.
Darkness appears,
till tomorrow, another splashing day.

Claire Keenan (10)
St Mary's Primary School, Killyleagh

THE SEA

The sea is a cat, small and grey,
He runs up and down.
He pounces on a gull.
He hits his tail against rocks,
He licks himself clean.
He goes here and there and then crash!
He bumps into a sandcastle and then retires to strike again.

Michael Gregge (9)
St Mary's Primary School, Killyleagh

WHAT CAN YOU DO WITH A YO-YO?

You can do tricks
like make it spin
around the world or even
walk the dog or you can
bake some bread
hit people on the head
you can use it to spread
use it to hammer in a nail
or make it go as slow as a snail
you could make a chair
or make it float in mid air
make it so famous
and meet Pope Seamus
make up a name or
give it a lion's mane
make it burn in the night
or could we make it fight
put it in an aeroplane
send it to Spain
and never show its face again
if it comes back
I'll tell Jack
to put it away
somewhere it can stay.

Matthew Nelson (9)
St Mary's Primary School, Killyleagh

THE CALL OF SPRING

Something told the waking bear
it was time to stretch,
time to get up from its nap
to look for food and drink.

Ambling along across the grass
looking for some food,
finding hardly any berries
because there are so few left.

Something told the new buds
it was time to burst,
time to spring up into blossoms
in the spring's warm earth.

Safe inside their winter home
with a soft breeze blowing,
they push up through the dark brown soil
then pop out a beautiful blossom.

But something told the migrating birds
winter's gone, spring is here.
We're calling you, come back!
The birds have heard our cry
I can see them glide across the sky.
They're coming home!

Luke Turley (8)
St Mary's Primary School, Killyleagh

SPRING'S SONG

Something told the birds
it was time to return.
Time to come back
from the hot country.

Something told the birds
it was time to find a mate
and lay its eggs
in a nest.

Something told the animals
it was time to wake up
and stretch their arms
from their long sleep.

Something told the flowers
it was time to grow,
to push up through the soil
and spread their petals.

Ryan Stavely (9)
St Mary's Primary School, Killyleagh

SEASHORE

Scuttling crabs run over the shore,
as cold sea tides come in.
Slowly and calmly the tide jogs in,
to find not a soul nor sinner,
except screeching gulls,
circling overhead
till dusk turns to dawn,
reaching for the day.

Stacey Woodside (9)
St Mary's Primary School, Killyleagh

THE SEA

See how the waves crash upon the rough rocks, where spiders crawl.
Taste the tangy salt water in your mouth.
Buoys floating side by side, ships go past.
Water fills the caves while I explore rock pools.
Catching fish is good fun.
Walk along the jetty observing the fish,
Paddle aimlessly in the water.
Examining the seaweed and the sea life.
The coastguard's out and what . . .
A swimmer in the prohibited side.
The coastguard saved him, thank heavens for that!
The sun shines and I dream.

Antoinette Quinn (10)
St Mary's Primary School, Killyleagh

THE SEA

The sea is like a baby's cradle,
Rocking to and fro,
You hear a quiet hush, hushing,
Sometimes it is slow,
Sometimes it is rushing,
It twirls around the rocks and
Trickles in the shells,
It's like a giant crystal in the morning when the sun is out.
At night it swishes calmly back and forth.

Anneka Perry (10)
St Mary's Primary School, Killyleagh

PRISON BIRD

I look through the gold prison bars
to find a blue parrot being held captive.

He fills the cells with loudness
and scrapes going down the
long metal bars.

As its eyes stare at me
like small beady stones,
a crack of a nut, a ting
of a door,
he is set free and hovers
right above me ready to leap
on my shoulder to make peace
and be my friend.

Christina Woodside (11)
St Mary's Primary School, Killyleagh

AUTUMN

Autumn's leaves on the ground,
Chestnuts falling from the trees.
Children run with laughter,
They walk without fear.
The trees are full of fruit,
For animals to come and eat.
Grown-ups jump on the leaves,
With so much happiness.
It really is a lovely sight,
For anyone to see.

Therese McGee (10)
St Mary's Primary School, Kircubbin

ANGEL-PIG

My kind of pet is a pig.
But not a normal, everyday pig,
Oh no, that's where you're wrong,
My pet is a one-of-a-kind.
You won't see her anywhere else,
She has two wings, one yellow, one orange,
She has green ears, special ones too.
Have you figure her out yet?
Well, I'll tell you,
She's a flying pig.
Ever heard the expression 'And pigs can fly'?
That's what she is, my little Angel-Pig,
A pig that *can* fly.
Her face is big and round, with purple spots on it.
She flies up, up, up to the high heavens,
Then down, down, down again below.
She sunbathes too, sometimes.
She loves rolling around in the mud,
Getting dirty.
She is the best pet anyone could wish for.
I absolutely adore her,
And I will always have a place in my heart for her.

Therese Hoeritzauer (11)
St Mary's Primary School, Kircubbin

APPLE

An apple is a shiny fruit,
It shines all day and night,
In the spring it starts to grow,
In autumn it drops off the trees
And we eat it.

Andrew Ritchie (10)
St Mary's Primary School, Kircubbin

PEACE

I want peace,
You want peace,
Why do we not have peace?
I abhor terrorists, their killings and beatings.
With them, there will be death.
Will you please stop the violence?
I beg you please,
Stop the killing,
Stop the beatings, stop the shootings.
It's on the news,
The killing and the violence.
The politicians are working hard
Nothing is changing.
I pray for peace
I hope for peace,
Please will everyone help make peace?

Tony Bowman (10)
St Mary's Primary School, Kircubbin

MONKEYS

Red bums on baboons,
Big hands on gorillas,
Hairy faces on orang-utans,
Spiky spider monkeys,
Fluffy teddy monkeys,
I love them all,
But at last, chimpanzees,
My favourite of them all.

Kathryn McNamara (10)
St Mary's Primary School, Kircubbin

THE BABY POLAR BEAR

He is just born.
One little polar bear, just one little bear born.
His mother names the cub,
She says to her husband,
'What about Ben?'
When he is a couple of days old,
He wants to explore that little, white, snowy place out there.
He is scooting through the snow, stepping on every bit of soft ice.
The polar bear leaves baby foot marks as a track,
He is so cute and adorable!
I see him floating across the cold Atlantic Sea on a block of ice.
I'm the one that could watch a polar bear family all day long,
On a little land of their own.

Conor Woods (10)
St Mary's Primary School, Kircubbin

SPRING

Spring is my favourite time,
When winter is left far behind,
The snow, the wind and rain,
Won't be back again,
Not for some time anyway.

The trees will turn green,
Small flowers will be seen,
The grass will grow tall,
Not as high as the wall.
My dad will be out
'Keep off, I'm mowing the grass' he'll shout.

Sarah Taylor (11)
St Mary's Primary School, Kircubbin

BACK TO REALITY

As I look at the clock,
And the 10 o'clock news begins,
I scratch myself and let out a yawn.
I go upstairs,
And drop with a thud,
Before I even get to my room.

I am in Slumberland,
The land of dreams and nightmares.
I float on a magic carpet,
I see children and happiness,
And I smile.
This is the life!

All of a sudden my carpet disappears,
I am in the nightmare section of Slumberland.
I see the devil burning bodies.

I am going to be killed,
Shot down in my dreams,
I am being chased by a van.
I run and run until,
I am forced off a cliff.

Shh!
Everything is silent.
I am back on the stairs again.
It's 7 o'clock.
Mummy is here to wake me up.
No more Slumberland for another night.

Thank God!

Shona Killen (10)
St Mary's Primary School, Kircubbin

THE WORLD

The world to me is a magnificent thing,
With different seasons, like winter and spring,
It contains creatures
Big and small, with lots of different features.
It's got day and night,
Which brings great light,
Days are sometimes good, sometimes bad,
Even very sad.
The weather's always changing,
When our lives are rearranging.
Red, brown, green and blue,
Make up the skies, seas, along with me and you.
The one man I'd like to thank is God,
If it wasn't for Him,
Our lives would be dim,
His people may not be great,
But I thank God they're my mates.

Eugene Gilmore (11)
St Mary's Primary School, Kircubbin

MY DAD

There's water dripping off the ceiling,
Water slithering down the walls,
Water on the doors,
And water on the floors.
Whenever Dad takes a bath
There's water *everywhere!*

Clare Quinn (9)
St Mary's Primary School, Kircubbin

BONZO

He chewed at the table,
Tore a hole in my shirt,
I shouted so loudly,
And he looked so hurt.

I said I was sorry,
And felt really bad,
After all he's only a pup,
And he looked so sad.

I went to the cupboard,
And some polish I found,
I covered the scrape,
That was made by the hound.

I told him if he did not be good,
He'd be locked in his kennel,
Without any food.

Philip McMaster (10)
St Mary's Primary School, Kircubbin

FRIENDS POEM

Friends, friends,
Stick together,
In everything they do,
Friends, friends,
Stick together,
No matter what they do.
Friends, friends,
Friends forever.

Cheryl Masterson (11)
St Mary's Primary School, Kircubbin

SMOKING

Puff, puff all day,
The more you smoke
The more you pay
Price is high
Health is low
Stop now, before you go.

Young is beautiful,
My age I guess,
The mirror is clear,
But my face is a mess.

Yellow teeth, tatty hair,
Spots on my face,
Everywhere.

Mark Morrison (11)
St Mary's Primary School, Kircubbin

MY DOG, MAX

My dog, Max
he's a really dirty dog.
He'll roll in muck
after his bath.

He barks all night . . .
and never stops.

He eats till he drops
and licks the bowl clean.
My dog, Max . . .
He's a really dirty dog!

Sarah Torney (11)
St Mary's Primary School, Kircubbin

PRAY FOR PEACE

Pray, come on, pray for peace,
That everyone may be friends,
That everyone can go out knowing it's safe
This world might come to an end.

Pray, come on, pray for peace,
Shed those tears and bring out hope,
Show your faith and justice
This world might come to an end.

Stop the killing and shooting,
The murders and the bomb scares,
Let's all pull together and make this world
A better place to live in.
If you do, you have found peace in your heart.

Joanne Kelly (11)
St Mary's Primary School, Kircubbin

MY PET CAT

My pet cat is my best friend,
His fur is warm and soft,
Like a blanket in my bed.
He is brown and black,
With a snow-white chest.
He smells like fresh clothes,
Out of the wash.
I hear a little cry,
Out on the window sill for his dinner.
I love my pet cat.

Conor Busuttil (10)
St Mary's Primary School, Kircubbin

CLASH OF THE GIANTS

Man Utd race out into the park,
Waiting for them is the crowd,
Screaming, shouting, laughing.
The match finally kicks off,
The players set to their work,
The crowd rise from their seats.

Player to player, passing about,
Waiting for that great first goal.
Running around, imagining when it might come,
Suddenly, out of the blue,
Comes a player all by himself,
He sprints towards the net,
Takes a shot!
The crowd become hysterical.

The fans wait, the players too,
Has he scored the goal?
The goalkeeper dives, but it's too late.
They've scored at last.
The crowds jump with joy.
The players congratulate the effort.
The scorer's swamped, clapped, embraced,
He has scored that vital goal,
A goal that will take them to the top!

Neill Caughey (11)
St Mary's Primary School, Kircubbin

SNAKE-A-RILLA

I'm a Snake-a-Rilla with long, hairy arms,
I can swim, I can fly by the use of charms.
I make loud sounds and roar like a gorilla,
That's why I'm named Snake-a-Rilla!
I hiss like a snake, which everyone hates,
But I don't care,
I'm not the only noisy animal out there!
My name is very strange,
It's well out of range!
I can slither, I can swing from tree to tree,
And when I land with a thud, they know it's *me!*
I live in the jungle with all my mates,
I sing weird songs, which they all hate.
At the end of the day, when I'm tired and deadbeat,
I rest in my bed and put up my feet!

Kerry Finnegan (11)
St Mary's Primary School, Kircubbin

THE OLD AND CREEPY MANSION

The old and creepy mansion,
Yeah, that old creepy thing.
It's been abandoned for fifty years,
And all the entrance is
Is a couple of rusty piers.
My mum says never to go near the place,
She says it's a nightmare case.
I'm going around tonight with a couple of my mates,
Maybe this time we'll pass the gates.

Ross Torney (10)
St Mary's Primary School, Kircubbin

MY PET HIPPO!

I have a pet, an unusual pet,
Who is purple and green.
He is really fat and he eats all day.
Can you guess?
I didn't think so.
It is a hippo!
He rolls about in the mud all day,
And he takes me to the park to play.
One day he ate and ate and ate,
Until we had to take him to the vet.
When we got there we couldn't get him
through the door!
We pushed and pushed but the hippo
didn't go through, he was stuck!
Then we got him out but now he has
a dent in his sides!

Cheryl Clarke (10)
St Mary's Primary School, Kircubbin

MY CAT THAT FLIES

My black and white cat,
Who likes to fly,
Around the house,
Around you, me, anyone who gets in her way,
She likes to fly with butterflies,
High in the sky,
Where the sun shines bright,
And the birds fly high,
Oh how she loves to fly.

Christina Murray (11)
St Mary's Primary School, Kircubbin

FLUFFA MONKA

I'm a fluffa monka with webbed feet and a beak,
I can fly up to the sky and don't forget, I can speak!
My friend got caught by a poacher sometime last year
And I can tell you, it's definitely my greatest fear,
I'm a very fluffy little thing, I almost look like a parrot,
I eat bananas, apples, lettuce and I love the odd carrot.
I swing from tree to tree all day long
And while I'm doing this I sing a sweet little song.
Sometimes I would come down and practise on my dancing,
But all the others say all I'm doing is prancing.
If you haven't guessed what I am yet, I'll spill the beans now
I'm half monkey, half parrot and to tell you the truth,
I don't know how!

Danny Fowler (10)
St Mary's Primary School, Kircubbin

THE 'FISH SNAKE'

I have a new friend,
who lives in a pond
His skin is all shiny,
and he is very long.

He moves through the water,
with a flick of his tail
The birds try to catch him,
but they always fail.

Fishermen try to catch him,
as they pull in their reel.
A 'Fish Snake' I call him,
his real name's an eel.

Jonathan Dougherty (11)
St Mary's Primary School, Kircubbin

My New Pet

My new pet is baby Kong,
Everything it does, it does it wrong,
It's a baby in distress,
And makes a mess,
I'm afraid it's half monkey,
So if you don't believe me, come and see,
It's a monkey telling a fib,
Its bottom half is soft and gentle,
But its top half, I'm ready to kill,
It's clumsy all around and makes quite a sound,
It crawls about,
Screams and shouts,
It's not my pet, it's my brother,
Which is very unfortunate for my mother,
If you want him, he's up for sale,
But I warn you, every hour he starts to wail.
So there you go, you know all about my new pet,
If you get him you'll get bottles and the whole set.

Sean Ennis (11)
St Mary's Primary School, Kircubbin

The Shark

The shark is big,
The shark if fierce,
The shark has a scaly body,
With really sharp teeth,
He could tear us apart in ten seconds.
As the shark looks at the boat above,
He suddenly thinks of fish.
He lurks around and spots one,
I really do feel sorry for that poor creature.

Gareth Finnegan (11)
St Mary's Primary School, Kircubbin

MILLENNIUM BUG

Scary, freaky, creepy,
black and brown its colour is,
its legs so long,
its mouth so big,
its hair so short,
the Millennium Bug is so weird and shocking!

Why oh why is it here?
why oh why did it appear,
with a screech, with a scream,
munching up my computer scheme?

Running here all day running there all night,
with electric it's looking to play,
where is it going next?
To gobble up the teletext.

Julie McGrattan (11)
St Mary's Primary School, Kircubbin

RABBITS

Twitching their noses in the air,
Faster than a tortoise and faster than a hare,
Hopping up and down,
Running in its hutch round and round,
Crunching and munching its cabbage leaves,
Rabbits are so friendly they would never deceive,
These lovely creatures,
Have wonderful features,
And they are nearly as smart as teachers!

Cathy Coyle (11)
St Mary's Primary School, Kircubbin

JACK FROST

When I went to bed last night
It came.
He came!
The one who makes winter what it is!
He's a cold person.
Has no heart at all.
He drops the snow.
He blows the wind.
He brings the frost.
He froze the puddles.
He froze our seat
Out in our garden.
He froze the path
That leads to our gate.
He froze everything around
Causing accidents.
He's bad and he's mean!
He's Jack Frost!

Stephanie Flynn (10)
St Patrick's Ballygalget, Portaferry

AN ICY WALK

I walk across the sea of white.
How beautiful it is!
Winter's icy fingers brush across my face.
This strange and new world
How unreal it seems!
Now the sun is rising.
This strange and new world is melting,
Until winter's icy fingers return.

Erin Healy (10)
St Patrick's Ballygalget, Portaferry

OLD

When I am old
I am going to drive around in a big, expensive car.
I'm not going to drink tea,
I'm going to drink Coke!
I'm going to run races
And play football with my grandchildren!
I am going to architecturally design my house
With an arcade room and playroom!
I am going to wear Nike and Adidas.
I'll spoil my grandchildren!
I will eat sweets and fries
And shepherds' pies.
I'll wear my hair
With lots of gel
When I am old!

Lawrence Smyth (10)
St Patrick's Ballygalget, Portaferry

MY AUNTY CHRISSY

My Aunt Chrissy sits in her chair
Watching the cows in the field.
Sometimes she looks over at her old house.
She tries to help Lillian to do things.
She hobbles on her walking stick.
Her skin is wrinkled.
Her legs are stiff.
Her hands are swollen.
I wonder what it feels like
To be old.

Vincent Toner (10)
St Patrick's Ballygalget, Portaferry

THE WIND

This morning the wind was moaning loudly,
Screaming, screeching,
Moaning,
Charging like a bull,
Ruining anything in sight,
Leaving a trail of ruins
To mark where he has been,
Searching for something to mark his victory.
He comes silently.
He rampages like a bull,
Knowing he can't be stopped,
Forcing rain to hit the wall,
Forcing trees to sway.
Yelling,
Shouting,
I am the king!

Michael Brennan (10)
St Patrick's Ballygalget, Portaferry

WIND

The wind sweeps through the trees
Rain slashes up against the windows
Children can't go out
Leaves fly up with the wind
Higher and higher
Making its way anywhere.
     I
        hate
          wind.

Aidan McKeating (11)
St Patrick's Ballygalget, Portaferry

LONELINESS

I feel lonely now.
I don't have my brother.
At nights I feel lonely having no one to talk to.
No one to muck about with,
Or mess with.
I hate being lonely.
I can't stand it!
Loneliness is a horrible thing.
You don't feel complete.
If the stars are out
I always pick a few stars.
I talk to them.
I pick one for Ryan,
Uncle Peter, Granda and Amy-Beth.
I also pick a couple more for those
Whom I didn't really know,
But were in my family.

Marie-Therese Coffey (10)
St Patrick's Ballygalget, Portaferry

FROST

Frost is crunchy.
It shines and looks like glitter.
I will slide on the frost.
How beautiful it looks!
If I touch it.
I am cold,
Shivering.
It will dry
When the sun comes out.

Mary-Bridget Murray (11)
St Patrick's Ballygalget, Portaferry

MY GRANNY

My granny is an old person.
She has wrinkled skin
like the bark of a tree.
She hobbles about.
But my granny is a sporty person!
She wears a Nike jumper,
Nike trousers and Nike Air Max Tri-ax trainers.
She has a Honda car
And speeds about the streets,
Even though she is an old person!
When I am old
I will be the same as my granny!

Paul Keith (9)
St Patrick's Ballygalget, Portaferry

THE WINTER WOLF

The winter wolf
is no ordinary wolf.
As he prowls
he leaves behind
a trail of frost.
As he howls
I see patterns on my window.
Frost freezes every shadow
with his piercing cold breath.
He is the winter wolf!

T P Harte (10)
St Patrick's Ballygalget, Portaferry

FOOTBALL MAGIC

I would love to play football and score lots of goals,
Just like Man Utd's Paul Scholes.
I would not be shy
When people watch me on Sky,
Going into the match
In my old shorts that need a patch.

A player in my team
Didn't turn up because he had a bad dream.
I thought to myself what else could go wrong.
But then the other side scored and their fans sang a song.
Here comes a cross, oh yes the ball's mine,
I shoot and it goes over the line.

It's a goal!

Gerard Collins (8)
St Patrick's Boys' Primary School, Downpatrick

DRAGONS AND KNIGHTS

Long, long ago, there were
So many dragons and knights,
Having so many battles and fights.

Probably so many knights were
Falling, so many kings kept
Calling, calling, calling.

The dragon wasn't defeated,
But a king found a knight,
That was so bright,
He could kick the dragon
Out of sight.

Daniel Mageean (8)
St Patrick's Boys' Primary School, Downpatrick

SCHOOL

School, school,
I always have to go to school,
It is definitely not a place
Where you could play pool.

I wished school would be crazy,
So you could do anything,
A place where you didn't have to
Sing sing sing sing sing.

Oh, no, that horrible teacher's coming,
That filthy and dirty witch,
If only if I could,
I'd throw her in a ditch.

Ouch! That football
it hit me on the head,
Oh! Safe at last,
I am now in bed.

Neil Morgan (8)
St Patrick's Boys' Primary School, Downpatrick

THE TIME OF CHAOS ...

As I sit looking out of my window,
I see a beast of no gender.
This beast slowly creeps along
Stripping all of life.
It leaves but ice snow.

As death creeps over the nation,
A piercing cold is but the tip
Of the iceberg.
The air that I breathe
Feels like daggers ripping my lungs apart.

Now it begins. Raging ice ravages the land.
Deadly snow blinds the eyes of travellers.
The creeping mist conceals hidden dangers.
The mighty wind destroys all in its path.

Now we near the end of a time when chaos rules.
But effortlessly, it throws one final attack.
Torrential flooding is the end,
But when a bitter cold enters the air,
Nine months from now the cycle begins again.

Darryl Mason (10)
St Patrick's Boys' Primary School, Downpatrick

WINTER

At last, I'm here.
Yes yes yes!
I nip your toes
With my frosty teeth.
Wrap up warm, I'm out tonight.
I cover the world in ice and snow.

My crown is cold to the touch
With beautiful red and blue diamonds
Ready to touch.
My long icy beard, silver with ice.
My long icy fingers old and cold
To freeze your soul.
With my old icy body,
Silver and mean
Yes, that's me *winter!*

Michael McCrissican (10)
St Patrick's Boys' Primary School, Downpatrick

DING DONG DING DONG

Ding dong ding ding *dong!*
The weather goes bing bong.
It cracks and clanks
All day long!
The sun comes out and
It all turns to song.
The streams glow to
The river's flow.
The floods make the streams
That gleam.
I wonder if floods hurt your taste buds,
If the flood turns to mud?

Rónán Kernan (7)
St Patrick's Boys' Primary School, Downpatrick

MOTHER EARTH

My air is all polluted,
Who do I blame that on?
My water is all polluted,
Who do I blame that on?
My ears will hardly hear anymore,
Who do I blame that on?

Who invented aerosol cans
That punched a hole in the ozone layer?
Who invented cars
Which brought pollution in the air?
Who started dumping
Which polluted all the waters?

Who or what did all of these things?
Was it all the cars?
Was it all the fire?
Was it all the factories?
Was it the aerosol can?

No, the destroyer is man.

Mark Magee (10)
St Patrick's Boys' Primary School, Downpatrick

WEATHER MAKES SOME FANTASTIC SOUNDS

Weather makes some fantastic sounds like . . .
The rain pitters and the ice glitters.
The snow *crunches* and *bunches*
All up in piles.
The thunder *looms* and *booms.*
Lightning *cracks* and *smacks.*
The sun *glows* and *grows*
Until it *shines.*
I wonder if a bee
Likes the sun
Or the bird in a tree
Or a fish in a pond.
Well I know that's me.

Mark Slavin (8)
St Patrick's Boys' Primary School, Downpatrick

AUTUMN IS . . .

Crispy leaves russet and brown
All falling down to the ground
Some are crunchy, rough and ripped
Each tree is different
Like oak, beech, sycamore and horse chestnut too
You find acorns, conkers and beech nuts
They're gliding, dancing
Tumbling to the ground
You see the colourful carpet
Of leaves on the green grass
You hear crunching, crackling
As you step into the leaves

As the birds fly to Africa
The sky is getting darker
They get ready for their flight
To find the shining sunlight

The bonfire's smoke is puffing
Twirling and curling
Into the sky
The farmer cuts golden sheaves of corn
The smell of blackberry jam
And pies you just cannot resist
Squirrels start to hibernate
For the winter.

Philip Annett (8)
St Patrick's Boys' Primary School, Downpatrick

HELL ON EARTH

Grrr go the diggers ripping down forests
The hum of the noise is music to the workers' ears,

Mother Nature is getting angry
She rains and rains so work is cancelled.

Thank God! You stopped for two years. Thank God!
When will this madness stop?
Please, please, the pain, the agony.

Stop polluting the world,
Don't destroy the Earth.

Stop! Stop I tell you! Thank God.

Brian Scott (10)
St Patrick's Boys' Primary School, Downpatrick

I WISH I WISH

I wish I wish
For a million wishes,
So I can wish for
A brown horse so I can ride
Down a hill with the wind blowing in my face.
I could wish I was Peter Pan
So I could fly and fight Captain Hook.
I wish I could go to Disneyland every day
And have a lot of fun.
I wish I was a bird so I could see
Everything from above.
I wish I had a green car so I could drive very fast.

Kieran Murphy (9)
St Patrick's Primary School, Ballynahinch

SHOPPING

I really hate shopping
Going from stall to stall
Every time I go there
Something always seems to fall

My sister and I always play a game
Racing the trolleys from lane to lane
Whenever we do this it's always the same
And I always manage to get the blame

Sainsbury's, Tesco's and Woolworth's too
You would think there'd be something else to do
So what I am trying to tell you today
Is *please,* please give us something to play.

Darren Trimby (10)
St Patrick's Primary School, Ballynahinch

I LOVE MUSIC!

I love music
Listen to me sing!
Outside, inside
Very tunefully.
Every minute of the day
Music is my life!
Upstairs, downstairs
Sing, sing, sing!
I love music
Can't you guess?

Maeve McCauley (9)
St Patrick's Primary School, Ballynahinch

IF I WERE A CAT

If I were a cat
I would be the cutest thing
You have ever seen.

If I were a cat
I would have black and orange stripes
With big green eyes
That could see through the night.

If I were a cat
I would have a very long tail
I would have the most beautiful whiskers
That I could use to see
If I could fit through a hole.

If I were a cat
I would run so fast
I would catch all the mice
I would have very long arms with paws
With very sharp claws.

Julie Murray (9)
St Patrick's Primary School, Ballynahinch

FISH

Fish, there are all different kinds
There's flat ones, round ones and many more.
Some can be scary, some can be weird,
Some can be slimy,
But don't be scared to touch them,
They're harmless!

Rebecca McCann (9)
St Patrick's Primary School, Ballynahinch

CARS

Come for an hour,
And bring your car,
So I can see,
What yours might be.

It could be a Mini or maybe a Ford,
But don't you worry I won't get bored.

I love them all,
Big or small,
The way they look,
Will have me hooked.

Show me your key,
It's so classy,
I sit behind the wheel,
And as a king I feel.

Cormac Judge (9)
St Patrick's Primary School, Ballynahinch

THE FUTURE

Instead of cars, jetpacks
Instead of lorries, limousines
Instead of buses, solar powered cars
Instead of motorbikes, flying cars

Instead of schools, education at home
Instead of beds, nice soft floors to sleep on
Instead of money, everything was free
Instead of video recorders, a cinema at home.

Gregory Bonner (9)
St Patrick's Primary School, Ballynahinch

BROTHERS

Brothers, brothers, they just appear,
Younger and older they're always here.
Making noise and a lot of mess,
I long to see them less and less.

I need my space, I really do,
I have to sometimes queue, even for the loo.
My toys are precious, they should be mine,
I have to give them up! Every time!

Brothers, brothers they're always there,
Pulling and tugging even on my long hair.
I long for silence, it's very rare,
But I love them really and do sometimes care.

Louise Rooney (9)
St Patrick's Primary School, Ballynahinch

STARS

A burning fire in the sky
Brighter than brightest light
This beautiful shining light
Shining in the midnight sky
Watching over us

A burning fire in the sky
Shining brighter than the moon
Guiding us on our path
Shining in the midnight sky.
Watching over us.

Stephanie Jones (9)
St Patrick's Primary School, Ballynahinch

MY FAVOURITE SUBJECT

My favourite subject is science
Where I learn about nature's delights
I study about tigers and lions
And read of wonderful sights.

Electricity it flows in a circuit
You use it for light and for heat
It makes everything work in the kitchen
And it's useful for cooking your meat.

Water is the lifeblood of nature
It can exist as steam or as ice
But when it rains in the summer
I think it is not very nice.

Flowers are God's decorations
Their colour and smell are pure
And when you are feeling quite awful
To see them will give you a cure.

Now the science of nature is brilliant
With the bushes and massive tall trees
That provide a good home for the birdies
And rustle and sway in the breeze.

Sinéad Marmion (9)
St Patrick's Primary School, Ballynahinch

WHEN I GROW UP

When I grow up I'm going to be
A River dancer
That River dancer will dance
With pride and joy
That's me!

When I grow up I'm going to do
A degree in maths
That's me!
I know I have the courage.

Rebecca Smyth (9)
St Patrick's Primary School, Ballynahinch

BROTHERS

Brothers, brothers, I have four,
They're more active than a wild boar.
Their ages fall from twelve to one,
No wonder I've a thin Mum!

Let's start with the oldest, Patrick, he's tall and thin,
Some day I'll throw him into the bin.
He likes football, and so do I,
It's all great fun till I get hit in the eye.

Barry, he's next, he's in P3,
I remember when he couldn't reach my knee.
He giggles, laughs and dances,
And thinks there's a country called Pances.

Colum is the one who likes to be in charge,
To get past me he has to barge.
He had many curls, when he was a lad,
Now they're all gone, and that's not bad!

Peter the baby smiling and happy,
Some day they will run out of nappies!

Brothers, brothers, I have four,
And I don't need anymore!

Gerard Higgins (9)
St Patrick's Primary School, Ballynahinch

TELEVISION

I love telly, it's usually fun
It normally has something good on.
I like Friends and Father Ted too
If you watch it, it will humour you.

Sometimes it's boring so I play outside
Or when the news is on we always fight.
Dad wants this and Una wants that
And then there is Shauna
I want to hit with a bat.

But when Sunday comes
Everything's fine
And Mum and Dad sip at their wine.
At this time I'm out playing
But when I come in it's a lovely setting.

On school days when I come home
We watch Neighbours and Home and Away.
Then on Mondays it's even better 'cause
The Simpsons is on and Homer's always fatter.

Now it's weekend and school is over,
If you want to know what happens,
Read this poem over!

Clare Higgins (10)
St Patrick's Primary School, Ballynahinch

THERE'S A MAN . .

There's a man who lives at the end of my street,
His window's always shiny, his garden's always neat.
In summer he sits in his stripy deckchair,
Enjoying the sun and fresh summer air.

He tells us stories about his life,
Like the countries he's been to and where he met his wife.
But my favourite story without a doubt,
Is the one he told me when no one else was about.
It was a story of how his dad fought in World War One,
'There was a knock on the door and he was handed a gun.'

So off he went as any man would
To defend his country as any man should.
With a brave smile on his face and a tear in his eye,
He kissed me and my brothers and sisters goodbye.

Life was hard when Dad was away,
But Mum kept telling us 'He'll be back some day.'
I used to cry at night to Mum,
'It's okay son, your dad'll be home when the war has been won.'

It was four years now, to the very day since Dad left in 1914,
A lot had changed and I had grown,
As it remained to be seen,
'cause the look on his face when he walked through the door,
was enough to make you cry.
The same brave smile and the tear in his eye,
Hadn't moved from the day he'd said goodbye.

Christopher Rice (9)
St Patrick's Primary School, Ballynahinch

ANIMALS

There are so many kinds of animals
Big ones, small ones, thin ones and fat ones.
Dolphins are my favourite,
Through the sea they swim,
It seems as if they are smiling
Though they really are quite grim.
Next would come the King of Beasts,
Yes, you've guessed,
The lion has to come next,
Who quietly feeds upon the kill.
He has a tasty feast.
If you hurt an animal, think twice before you do,
Don't try to hurt them just be kind.
If you only want to pet them,
I'm sure they won't mind.

Natasha O'Connor (10)
St Patrick's Primary School, Ballynahinch

MY HOBBY

My hobby is Irish dancing
I really do adore
I go there every Saturday
To learn new steps and more
Whether it is a reel, jig or hornpipe
I do not really mind
For the Ulster Championships
To battle them out in Bangor town
Ballycastle to Newcastle to Newtonards
To Ballymena each year.

Caroline Davey (9)
St Patrick's Primary School, Ballynahinch

FOOTBALL

I like to play football
Man United is my team
To play beside Giggsy
Is my ultimate dream.

I'd like to be a striker
And score lots of goals
Like the ones that are scored
By Beckham and Scholes

I think Peter Schmeichel
Is the best of the lot
He makes it look easy
When he saves a shot

So when I grow up
It's Old Trafford for me
There's no other place
That I'd rather be

Just to hear all those thousands
Chanting my name
And to lift up the cup
At the end of the game

To me it would be
The best of the rest
And then I would know
That I'd really be blessed.

Christopher Molloy (10)
St Patrick's Primary School, Ballynahinch

MY LIFE

My life is full of wonderful things,
My mum, my dad and sister.
They always help me throughout my life.

My life is full of ups and downs.
Happy times and sad times.
Happy times when I get what I want
And sad times when I don't get what I want.

I like my home and my family.
I like my friends who play with me.
My school is a fun place,
Where I go every day.
It helps me to learn and sometimes play.

Gerard O'Hare (10)
St Patrick's Primary School, Ballynahinch

GROWING BRINGS JOY

I grow like a flower
To have lots of power
I grow on
Just like a swan
I am tall
A mouse is small
You grow each day
Just like us in every way.

Tammy Quinn (10)
St Patrick's Primary School, Ballynahinch

QUIET, QUIET!

Quiet, quiet goes the little mouse.
Quiet, quiet it scampers about the house.
Quiet, quiet give me some cheese.
Quiet, quiet nah ah say please!

Quiet, quiet goes the big cat.
Quiet, quiet it is very fat.
Quiet, quiet give me some mice.
Quiet, quiet nah ah be nice!

Quiet, quiet goes the little bird.
Quiet, quiet it sings tweet tweet.
Quiet, quiet give me some seeds.
Quiet, quiet nah ah be sweet!

Victoria Noade (9)
St Patrick's Primary School, Ballynahinch

SUNFLOWERS

Sunflower . . .
Slightly twisted stalk
Yellow petals in a yellow circle
Leaves growing up the stalk so beautifully.
Growing,
     Growing,
          Growing
So high
Crying for water or they will die.

Conor Nugent (10)
St Patrick's Primary School, Newry

MY LITTLE BROTHER

My little brother is tall and thin
He has blond hair and a wee chin
His front tooth is missing
And he has a big bad grin.

He is boss, he gets all things his own way
If not, there is hell to play.
I am sick of Barney, Phill and Lill.
Action Man I could kill,
Scattered here and scattered there.
A room of my own I would prefer.

To the attic I may go
And run my own show.
And get my turn on the computer and say
Who can have a go.
My sweets would be safe
Peace I would have.

Matthew Carberry (10)
St Patrick's Primary School, Newry

MY BROTHER

My brother Ryan has bright blond hair,
he finds it hard to sit on a chair,
he's seven years old, and sometimes bold,
but other times he does what he's told.
Sometimes late at night we have a pillow fight.
Now and then when I am sad,
he tickles me and makes me glad,
to have a brother called Ryan.

Ryan Conlon (7)
St Patrick's Primary School, Newry

SUNFLOWER

My sunflower grows tall
taller than me,
with bright yellow petals
for everyone to see.
Its tall twisted stalk,
blows in the wind
Its head hangs low
when the sun is dim.

Sean Evans (10)
St Patrick's Primary School, Newry

MY LITTLE SISTER

My little sister is a pain
She always wants to join the game
Even though she is too young
Sometimes, I let her play along
At times she is very bold
But she has a heart of gold.

Danielle Brennan (9)
St Patrick's Primary School, Newry

MY SISTER

I have a sister called Della
Sometimes she's not a bad bella
But when she's not nice
She can give you a fright
And that's my sister called Della.

Jade Teelan (9)
St Patrick's Primary School, Newry

TINKERBELL

I have a cat
Who is very fat,
Her name is Tinkerbell.
She hisses at dogs,
Scrabs at frogs
And I love her very well.
She's black and amber
And is very tender.
She is almost five years old.
She jumps on me,
Scrabs my knee
But I love her more than gold.

Hannah Green (10)
St Patrick's Primary School, Newry

SUNFLOWERS

S is for the lovely sun
U is for under the soil
N is for the new flowers
F is for the sunflowers
L is for the leaves
O is for the ordinary flowers
W is for the water
E is for earwigs crawling in the soil
R is for all the raining days.

Karen Hanratty (9)
St Patrick's Primary School, Newry

MY BEST FRIEND

My best friend is a dog called Spider
He doesn't like storms
I don't either.
We have so much fun together
Especially in good weather.
He's as good as gold
Always does what he's told
He's my best friend forever and ever.

Leanne Rushe (10)
St Patrick's Primary School, Newry

MY COUSIN

I have a cousin called Aaron
Who does not like the name Darren
He is very crazy
But he is not lazy
He thinks he is tough
When he fights he is rough
And he always ends up in a huff.

Ciara Rushe (10)
St Patrick's Primary School, Newry

MY SUNFLOWER

It stands tall against the wall - my sunflower
Its beautiful brown face smiles in the sun
Its vibrant, golden petals soft to the touch
It is so elegant - my sunflower.

Gary Harte (10)
St Patrick's Primary School, Newry

SUNFLOWER

My sunflower stands so very tall
Staring over the garden wall.
She is so happy
When the sun comes out,
It really makes her petals stand out.
When visitors pull up at the garden gate
It's the scent of my sunflower that greets them first.
The scent is so sweet
It makes them look.
This makes my sunflower feel special
Which she really is of course,
I am so proud
That she is all mine.

Leona Quinn (10)
St Patrick's Primary School, Newry

SUNFLOWERS POEM

Standing tall, smiling face,
Thoughts of winter in another place.
Standing proudly with leaves
Spread out like arms,
This is part of the sunflower's charms.
Its stem is like a six-foot man,
Watching the sunflowers makes me feel calm.
Because it reminds me of holidays
With blue skies and sunny sun.
Its petals are like wee balls of fire.

Keelan Conlon (10)
St Patrick's Primary School, Newry

MY COUSIN

I have a cousin called Annie
She is nine years old
She has a dog called Bob
Who is as good as gold
She lives in Belfast City
Which is such a pity
Because it is so far away from me.

Aveen Donaldson (10)
St Patrick's Primary School, Newry

TREES

I love trees
I love them all
Fat or thin
Big or small
In the autumn
You will see
Withered leaves
Fall off the trees.

Aoife Boyle (10)
St Patrick's Primary School, Newry

TREES

Trees, trees, they blow in a breeze
Tall and slim
Small and fat
When a big wind comes
They all fall flat.

Geraldine Hearty (9)
St Patrick's Primary School, Newry

THE MILLENNIUM

The millennium is coming, it's very near,
Looking forward to an exciting year,
Walking down the busy street,
Everyone is rushing off their feet,
Shops are selling lots of stock,
On the 1st of January, it's time to rock!

The year 2000 is going to be
A very important year for me,
I'll be leaving primary school,
If I don't, I'd be a fool,
All the teachers I won't forget,
If I do, I could regret.

In the run up to the millennium
There will be a big fuss,
And in that year I'll be doing my eleven plus,
In this big year nearly everything will be changed.
Most of our lives will be disarranged,
For this year I cannot wait,
It's very fascinating, it will be great!

Claire Toner (10)
St Ronan's Primary School, Newry

SILLY, SILLY MILLENNIUM

The world will celebrate the millennium,
People will starve in the millennium.
Children will die in the millennium.
War will continue in the millennium.
Global warming will still happen in the millennium.
So what's all the fuss about the millennium.

Conall Starrs (9)
St Ronan's Primary School, Newry

MILLENNIUM

Parties, concerts, all night long,
we welcome in the year 2000.

The Third Millennium is arriving,
With fireworks and songs galore,
Fun like we've never had before.

Millennium Bugs, computer crashes,
Hours and hours of fun-filled bashes.

The Millennium Dome is such a success
And it even has an e-mail address.

As midnight of 1999 approaches,
We board our buses and coaches,
To ride into town,
For the big countdown.

10, 9, 8, 7, 6, 5, 4, 3, 2, 1
It's the new millennium!

Emiear McShane (10)
St Ronan's Primary School, Newry

MILLENNIUM DOME

The Millennium Dome is nearly made,
Come on everyone the drinks are paid
Be there early to get a good place
There'll be peanuts and drink, it's better than the Mace.
Ring a taxi because you'll be home late,
If you run out of money,
Tell them to put it on the slate!

Emma Strain (10)
St Ronan's Primary School, Newry

THE MILLENNIUM

10 Will the Earth be invaded by spacemen?
9 Let's celebrate with bottles of wine.
8 We'll stay up late.
7 Eleven o'clock now, only one more hour.
6 Tick, tick, tick, the minutes go by.
5 Let's enjoy!
4 Fill up the glasses more.
3 Will this be the end of me?
2 All the balloons are blown.
1 Everything's done!

Cheers and celebrations
The millennium has come.

Gavin Donald (10)
St Ronan's Primary School, Newry

THE MILLENNIUM

The millennium is the best time of year,
So enjoy yourself have some beer,
A thousand years have passed at last,
What a blast,
Festivals and parties.

The fun time of year, the *millennium,*
Has come again,
And have no fear,
Just cheer and cheer.

Ronan Hughes (10)
St Ronan's Primary School, Newry

MILLENNIUM 2000

Hip hip hooray, the millennium is here today.
Busy streets with people buying treats,
For their visitors to eat.

Fireworks bursting high in the dark sky,
Making babies and children cry.
Balloons and streamers everywhere you look,
With a multicoloured sky for luck.

Different coloured street lights, parades to entertain,
Other people thinking that we are definitely insane.

People up late at night, partying with all their might.
Children in the streets look surprised,
Wondering where this excitement lies.
With the parades so sparkly and amusements so loud,
People walking look so proud.

A big church celebration for when Jesus died 2000 years ago,
With choirs singing high and low.

Music on the streets, people dancing to the beat,
Thinking that this night was the *biggest ever treat.*

So the clock has just struck 12.00, and everyone shouts hooray,
10, 9, 8, 7, 6, 5, 4, 3, 2, 1, *the millennium is here today.*

Shenna Matthews (9)
St Ronan's Primary School, Newry

MILLENNIUM DOME

It is a place
big and round
wide and sound.
Strong as a rock
and wide as a lough.
It may look small
like a ball.
It is so big
and the best of fun
I'd love to go there
for a run.

I'll go through the lungs today,
out of the heart,
into the vessels,
round the body
out of the toe.
To and fro.

We'll be back
don't you know!

Owen O'Donnell (10)
St Ronan's Primary School, Newry

MILLENNIUM PARTY

A millennium party in the street
and people dancing on their feet.
With slippered joy and prancing shoe
why you can join the millennium too!
Everyone's cool and everyone rules,
the millennium parties in all the schools!

Stephen McStay (10)
St Ronan's Primary School, Newry

A GREAT SPIRIT

I wish I was a great spirit,
So I could spread my huge wings over the land,
And lift the world with my gigantic hands.

Everywhere my wings take me,
I'll be throwing the world up and down,
And then when I've finished.
I'll put it back safe and sound.

I'm so big and the world's so small,
I'll use it as a basketball.

Maybe when I'm finished,
I'll throw the world away.
Then I'll get Goliath and we'll go and play.

Ciaran Fox (8)
St Ronan's Primary School, Newry

MILLENNIUM 2000

The millennium, the millennium,
One thousand years have passed,
Since the Vikings died out last.
We will come to celebrate with a friend,
On New Year's Eve to the end.

At the very last second we will cheer,
Because the new millennium is here,
And in a thousand years to come,
It will be a new millennium.

Conor Daly (9)
St Ronan's Primary School, Newry

MILLENNIUM 2000

The year 1999
Is a very special sign;
It introduces the year 2000.

Hotels in a bustle,
Chefs and cooks in a hustle.
Everybody in their homes,
Talking about the Millennium Dome.

On the 31st December round midnight,
People will be staring in awe at the sight.
Up in the air, there'll be a firework display,
Everyone merry and gay.

Every nation,
In raptures and celebration.
Dancing on the streets,
Instruments tapping out beats.

No matter where you choose to be,
Whether it's by land, air or sea,
London, New York, Paris, Munich,
Will be drowning in the sound of music.

There's one thing I'd like to hear
Within this very special year.
War and violence will finally end
And everyone will be a friend.

Jonathan Philpott (9)
St Ronan's Primary School, Newry

MILLENNIUM CRAZY

The world is going crazy
For the millennium baby
While we'll be singing
The bells will be ringing
For the year *2000!*

The Millennium Bug might shut down your computer
But it won't destroy your future.
We'll be having parties and eating Smarties
At the biggest party *ever*
It will be a privilege for us to see
The turn of a century.

Happy New Year
The millennium is here!

Simon Hollywood (10)
St Ronan's Primary School, Newry

MILLENNIUM 2000

Millennium 2000 is a great celebration
It's a truly wonderful momentous occasion
To live in two centuries
Is surely a feat
But to have lived in three centuries
Is specially unique.

The threat of the bug and the Millennium Dome
Fireworks and parties at everyone's home
But what is the message the millennium brings
It's Lord Jesus' birthday
Our king of kings.

Fiona Flynn (9)
St Ronan's Primary School, Newry

GREAT MAGIC

I wish I was magic.
I could do anything.
Making magic slippers
Satin dresses
Even a magic ring.
I could fly round the world
With my magic wand
And glide over the little flowing pond.
I hope my wish comes true
I really, really do.
Because magic is a simple thing to do.
Wish, woo!

Cathy Cassidy (8)
St Ronan's Primary School, Newry

MINIBEASTS AMAZING!

Bungie-jumping beetles jumping into beer!
Having the time of their life.
Angry ants in posh petticoats!
Showing off with all their might.
Wailing woodlouse in woolly dresses!
Angry, angry as can be.
Wriggling worms dancing, dancing!
At the disco every night
Aren't minibeasts amazing!

Cliona Kane (8)
St Ronan's Primary School, Newry

CELEBRATION 2000

Come on let's have a party!
The millennium is here!
We'll dance and sing and roar and shout,
So come on over here.

There will be music,
Food, people lights.
Fireworks, festivals,
What a sight!

The clock strikes twelve,
There's magic in the air
As another millennium has gone by.
We hope for peace as people cry.

Sarah Tumilty (10)
St Ronan's Primary School, Newry

MR WORM

Mr Worm wiggles and slides.
Mr Worm has no eyes.
But Mr Worm has a mouth
To suck in soil in his delight.
Mr Worm lives underground
That is why he has no eyes.
Mr Worm is very slimy.
Mr Worm has no legs
So he only wiggles and slides.

Christopher Cunningham (8)
St Ronan's Primary School, Newry

MILLENNIUM 2000

Our joyous world is celebrating
As the clock strikes twelve.
If you're enjoying the fun
Don't keep it to yourself.

The computer virus,
The Millennium Bug
Is striking this very minute.
But if you're enjoying yourself
It won't bother you for a moment.

So enjoy yourself and
Party the night away
Because if you're bored
You'd need a little fun for a day.

James Patterson (9)
St Ronan's Primary School, Newry

MY MAGIC PLANS

I wish I was magic
To do anything
To have magic slippers
And to have magic dreams
When I will be lonely
I will make a new magic friend
And when we are together
Our friendship of magic
Will never, ever end.

Paula Gribben (8)
St Ronan's Primary School, Newry

CELEBRATION 2000

Millennium is coming soon
We'll have a party on the street all night long
With a disco and a song.

With fireworks banging in the air
And people happy everywhere.
Come and celebrate the 2000th year
It's the start of a new millennium.

New babies coming into the world around us
Hoping they'll be the first 21st century babies.
For me a new school, new friends and experiences too.

Millennium Bugs, new carpet rugs.
Peace, joy, love, hope and fun
There's something in the millennium for everyone.

Paul Burns (10)
St Ronan's Primary School, Newry

MILLENNIUM 2000

The millennium is coming soon,
Robbie Williams and his new tune.

The millennium baby on its way.
World-wide parties, songs and discos to this day.

The start of the next century!
Excitement, noise, love, peace, hope, laughter
And parades for all of the day.

Lisa Burns (10)
St Ronan's Primary School, Newry

CELEBRATION 2000

Bang! Crack! The sky goes boom!
The crowds shout and scream!
Altogether we now fulfil
Our year 2000 dream!

Food and drinks, party mad!
We celebrate with cheer,
Fireworks, discos, street parades,
And the pub is very near!

Who cares about the Millennium Bug?
So what if the computers go awry!
Right now, what we need to concentrate on,
Is excitement and fun, *hip hooray!*

Ruth Quinn (9)
St Ronan's Primary School, Newry

CELEBRATION 2000

The year 2000 is almost upon us.
Millennium is its title.
Fun and laughter will be had across the land,
While the world parties the night away.

Peace and happiness it will bring for evermore.
Love will be shared, despite the creed or colour or culture.

Here's to the millennium.
Hip hip hooray!

Niall Boyle (9)
St Ronan's Primary School, Newry

MILLENNIUM 2000

Millennium 2000 is a wonderful thing.
We can dance, shout and even sing.
We celebrate by having street parties,
Firework displays and parades.
I wonder what will happen in the next thousand years?

The fireworks glisten at night
And seeing them up in the sky is a beautiful sight.
The noise gives me a fright.

Street parties are so noisy but a lot of fun.
I hope there will be laughter for everyone.

But what about the lonely people
Who have nothing to celebrate?
Who will be the Millennium Baby?
The millennium, I hope it will bring
Peace, hope, love and happiness.

Colleen Breen (10)
St Ronan's Primary School, Newry

CELEBRATION 2000

I can't wait till the year 2000.
It's when fireworks explode everywhere
and we are partying in the street.

It will be the start of a new century.
Soon it will be an exciting event.

It's when the Millennium Bug goes round.
Oh, I can't - oh, I can't wait.
Oh, I can't wait till the year 2000.

Shane Barr (10)
St Ronan's Primary School, Newry

CELEBRATION 2000

Fireworks glow and trumpets blare,
A feeling of suspense is in the air.
The year 2000 is drawing near -
Who knows what will come with this long awaited year.

Peals of laughter can be heard everywhere,
Sing songs in the night.
It's time to look at this new year
In a completely different light.

What will the millennium do for mankind?
In the next 1000 years what will we find?
What are our dreams for this Planet Earth,
As we celebrate 2000 years from our saviour's birth?

Let's start this millennium with world peace,
So all fighting will immediately cease.
To all the poor and the starving let's give some hope -
So through our kindness with life they can cope.

So let the millennium celebrations start,
Let there be happiness in your heart.
Remember the good things we've learnt from the past
And let's all join together, united at last.

Claire Hegarty (9)
St Ronan's Primary School, Newry

CELEBRATION 2000

Celebration 2000 that's what we'll do,
Disco dancing in the street.
The excitement of the last few seconds
Some could have cold feet,
But this time we're gonna have some real fun!

Celebration 2000 that's what we'll do
Some of us might go mad
But sure you'll only see it once
Fireworks all around everywhere you go.
They're lighting up the sky with colours that glow.

Celebration 2000 that's what we'll do,
Have you heard of the Millennium Dome.
And as for that Millennium Bug
He could really annoy you devouring computers, fun.
But I'll say only one thing
Have a great time, I know I will.

Ruairi Digney (10)
St Ronan's Primary School, Newry

CELEBRATION 2000

For the year 2000
We built the Millennium Dome.
Everybody will celebrate.
We'll have a party at home.
There will be lots of noise
And parades in the streets.
The children will have discos
And plenty of sweets.

Naomi Boyce (9)
St Ronan's Primary School, Newry

CELEBRATION 2000

It's the night of the 31st December tonight.
Just count to ten and find a surprise before your very eyes.
1, 2, 3, 4, 5, 6, 7, 8, 9, 10.
Bang! Slam! Wow, there's fireworks, parties
It's so much fun, let it never end.
It's just like magic all the light from the fireworks.
But this doesn't end, for tomorrow there'll be
Parades and the winner of the Millennium Baby.
Sadly computers go back to the year 1000
Meaning PCs and Internets might lose their dates and records
But it's still great no matter what happens to the computers.

Tara McGovern (10)
St Ronan's Primary School, Newry

CELEBRATION 2000

The year 2000 is a time
When everyone drinks beer and wine.
The parties last all night long
Mixed with a mixture of excitement and fun.
People dance all night long
Also mixed with excitement and fun.
People rushing all around
Making a lot of noise and sound.
People are so rough today
They might give you a push or shove and say sorry.
The year 2000 is a time,
When everyone drinks beer and wine.

John McCabe (10)
St Ronan's Primary School, Newry

MILLENNIUM

The year 2000 is nearly here,
People are coming from far and near.
The Dome is built for all to view,
Old and young, babies too.
London is the place to be,
With everything exciting to see.
Big Ben will start the countdown,
With fireworks and dancing in every town.

Ross Mathers (10)
St Ronan's Primary School, Newry

SNAKES

Knobbly knees,
Cold heart.
Get this thing off me -
Before I barf!
Boiling in fear,
Shaking in fright.
Get this thing off me -
Before it bites.
Hand shaking,
Head spinning.
Get this thing off me -
Or I'll start to scream.
Soft voice,
In case it bites.
Set me free or -
I won't sleep for nights!

Narayan Kirk (10)
West Winds Primary School

VERTIGO

Brave height,
Couldn't go -
I just want to be down low!
Sweating,
Knees sore.
Please - don't let go!

Thumping heart.
Need to know -
'How far is it for me to go?'
Feel sick,
Really cold.
Someone told me I was doing good.

I *have* to do this -
I want to be brave.
When he counts, 1, 2, 3 . . .
I will bungee!

Lauren Doole (10)
West Winds Primary School

MILLENNIUM VISITOR

Woke up
In the middle of the night,
Hear a *bang!*
Saw a bright light.

Coming down,
To the ground,
A big spaceship -
Looking like a giant chip!

Alien popped out.
Was walking about,
Saw me clear
And called me *Dear!*

I screamed,
It vanished!
Spaceship whirled away.
I felt bad -
Please come back another day!

Rachael Crawford (9)
West Winds Primary School

THURSDAY

Thursday, oh Thursday,
Homework is short.
Chops for dinner tonight,
Yum, yum!
Thursday, oh Thursday,
You're sparkly and bright,
You're line dancing night.
You don't make me blue -
You make me feel gold.
Thursday, oh Thursday,
I really love you!

Kylie Martin (10)
West Winds Primary School

MY UNCLE

If my uncle were a bird
He would be a peacock
With his wide wings spreading.

If my uncle were a fruit
He would be a kiwi,
With tough brown skin
And soft green fruit inside.

If my uncle were a tree
He would be a pine tree
Tall and straight with
Sweet smelling cones.

Chloe Miller (11)
Windsor Hill Primary School

MY MUM

If my mum were an insect
She'd be a butterfly, with big bright wings
And flutter from flower to flower.

If my mum were a fruit,
She'd be an orange
All bitter and sweet inside.

If my mum were a car,
She'd be a Renault Scenic
Quick, comfy and nice and big.

Karen Butler (11)
Windsor Hill Primary School

THE WORLD DOWN BELOW

The octopus, in his coral palace,
Glaring at it with eyes full of malice.
He sits beneath the ocean blue,
Wondering what next to do.

Let us admire the anemone,
Beside him is a clownfish (not his enemy)
Other fish meet a nasty end,
But the clownfish is the anemone's friend.

Consider the ponderous whale,
Moving along with his great flat tail.
He feasts on krill and plankton and such,
And swallows the lot with hardly a touch.

Matthew McDowell (9)
Windsor Hill Primary School

MY MUM

If my mum were a flower,
She'd be a lily, tall proud and elegant,
with beautiful white petals, resting on a lily pad.

If my mum were a fruit
She'd be a strawberry,
Red, soft and sweet, a delight to eat.

If my mum was a part of the solar system,
She'd be the sun,
Giving light and warmth to everyone she sees.

Haroula Pasparaki (10)
Windsor Hill Primary School

My Mum

If she was a type of weather
She would be thunder,
For she has a loud voice
And never gives in.

If she were a dog,
She would be a Yorkshire Terrier.
For she is always talking
And is very hard to drag away
                    from a conversation.

If she were an insect
She would be an ant
For she always get things done
And is very hard working.

Jonathan Tate (10)
Windsor Hill Primary School

Clouds

What are the clouds?
Are they candyfloss?
Or are they cotton wool?
Or a giant's large pillow?
I just don't know.

Iain McMillan (9)
Windsor Hill Primary School